The Footprints of the Academician

By Fu Shouzhi

NORTH
AMERICAN BUSINESS
PRESS

First Printing: 2015

ISBN: 9781948915113

Life should be fervent.

You can't just lay idle

and you should accomplish something.

When life is still fervent,

you should lose no time to contribute to the motherland's strength and people's wealth!

——— Fu Shouzhi

Preface (I)

A Hard-working, Aspiring and Enterprising Academician

I am glad to read *The Footprint of the Academician* which is one of those rare good works over the years and the crystallization of tears, sweats and strenuous efforts in Academician Yingge's lifetime.

All his life he has seized every minute and every opportunity to be engaged in innovations. He has embraced different hardships and challenges of life with great passion such as his fight against wild boars and ferocious wolves in the virgin forest in northeast of China, and his meticulous training of students in universities. He cherishes every minute to conduct scientific researches and even risks his life in order to do his share to motherland construction. What's most admirable is his unremitting effort in learning new things and his self-denying spirit.

In addition to his lofty thinking of making more contributions to the country and his consummate techniques, he is brave to devote himself to scientific experiments at crucial moments, which is both moving and respectable. Great minds mature slowly. Although he's getting older, he has completed his book-- *The Footprints of the Academician* which is bound to be well received among Chinese people.

At the United Nations' WAPS Conference held in Antalya, Turkey, in November, 2010, he was elected as an academician of WAPS and won academician certificate and medal. What a noble honor in the world!

In July, 2010, he was invited to attend the 16th World Conference on Management Science held in Paris, France. He served as the vice chairman of the conference, which was a glory for Chinese people.

He didn't think it's the end of his fighting in life much as he had been given the academician title. Instead, he worked harder than before. He assumed many posts in different social fields and was a social activist. Besides, he was invited to visit Russia, France, Germany, Switzerland, Austria and Italy, etc. for academic exchanges. He tried to enrich himself by further studying the latest scientific achievements abroad so as to make greater contributions to his motherland.

He always bears the motto in mind, "Life should be fervent. You can't just lay idle and you should accomplish something. When life is still fervent, you should lose no time to contribute to the motherland's strength and people's wealth!"

These precious sincere words are no doubt an example of learning for the younger generation and enlightenment as well for other progressives.

The Footprint of the Academician shows outstanding brilliance, excellent writing skills, heart-warming and inspiring stories, exciting and thrilling plots, all of which makes readers reluctant to tear themselves away from it.

Vice President and Academician of WAPS: Chen Shengchang

Beijing March, 2012

Preface (II)

Great Mind of the Academician Matures Slowly

I am extremely delighted to read the book of *The Footprints of the Academician*! He is buried in studies in retreat and shows his wisdom in the prosperous period. Professor Yingge is an innovative Chinese scholar with agile thinking who accomplishes something lasting but lives a quiet life. Besides, he is a typical character who "integrates knowledge and action". His personalities of modesty, restraint, low profile in conducting himself and braveness in acting are outstanding.

Just look! His pioneering spirit, enthusiastic life and fight spirit of being brave to climb science peaks are admirable. He's elected as the vice president of Chinese nationality on World Conference on Management Science held in Paris, France. He has left the footprint of academician Yingge on the red carpet in Turkey, a foreign land. It's indeed the pride and glory of Chinese people and the glory of Jiaotong University as well.

People are on their trips in their lifetime and how to experience it? Different people have different choices. How does Professor Yingge become a well-known WAPS academician from an ordinary train driver? His way of success is as follows:

I. Diligent and Hard-working in Studies

The most precious thing is independence. Success lies in diligence. As long as you are diligent in reading, you can know the world; as long as you read famous works, you can comprehend objective rules; further exploration can reveal the truth; therefore, he can compose high-level works such as *Master Sun's Arts of War and Corporate Management Strategy* and *Study on Development of China's Productivity-- Based on Thought of Scientific Outlook on Development.*

II. Impart Knowledge and Educate People with Unremitting Efforts

When the wind blows right, the trees grow straight. When the dew is moist, the flowers bloom. It's his motto. He always regards imparting knowledge and educating people as his primary task, thus making his students grow up, become talents and achieve success as soon as possible. He is strict with himself and educate students with his own examples, thus demonstrating the personality charisma of a teacher. He convinces his students both sentimentally and rationally. Both he and his students benefit the teaching process. He trains them with his meticulous efforts. Many of students whom Professor Yingge has taught become political elites, academic masters and industrial & commercial tycoons.

III. Devoted to Scientific Researches and Climb New Heights

After leaving the university, he set up "Jiaotong University Dalian Kathrin Special Alloy Research Institute" whose purpose is to develop low-carbon economy and promote energy-saving & emission reduction under the instructions of scientific outlook on development, build a harmonious ecological environment and make scientific researches serve productivity. Through over 20 years' arduous efforts, he has developed a batch of key scientific research achievements.

In terms of metal surface engineering studies and development, his technology has been listed in the world's top ones. He becomes the first one to use high temperature wear-resisting technology in thermal power boilers and is well reviewed by foreign and domestic scholars.

At present, he has three national invention patents and four high-tech achievement awards. As an academician, he has realized his perfect life.

Looking back on the life trajectory of Professor Yingge, it has been like the rising of the sun and every step is exquisitely arranged. His past is just vivid on his mind: he deftly and cleverly fought against Japanese soldiers when he's young; he mustered his courage to save people in the Snowy Forest; he was hard-working and diligent in studies; he imparted knowledge and educated people with unremitting efforts; he was completely devoted to scientific researches and climbed new heights; he became well-known with his academician title. It could be seen that he's a person who can do great things and get somewhere with his great thinking and sagacious wisdom. He's a typical character who is consistent in words and actions, and indeed the treasure of the country.

The book of *The Footprints of the Academician* is going to be released on the market. It's a superb life memoir. Its literary style is refreshing and elegant, simplistic and unadorned. It's a good textbook to educate the next generation.

His book has the style of Da Ya just like the spring wind which can tolerate all things; it is as extraordinary and bright as the Autumn Floods.

I would like to write this preface for mutual encouragement.

Former Party Committee Secretary of Dalian Jiaotong University: Sun Yongchun

Beijing April, 2012

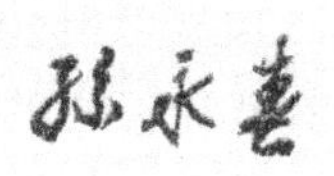

Preface (III)

The Enthusiastic Life of An Academician

He's a legend, I think.

I thought it must an autobiography book which isn't worth reading at the beginning! As a traditional literati in the humanistic field, I am not quite interested in science and technology. Those boring numbers and obscure terminologies sound horrible to me. What's unexpected is that the book has attracted me at the very start.

His childhood is permeated with hardships, coldness and famine as well as death threats. As a matter of fact, in the first half of his life, he has experienced lots of narrow escapes but he survived in the end. "As long as he can have his dream come true, he won't regret even if he dies nine deaths"! This warrior whose eyebrows spread like those of a judge always says the King of the Hell doesn't like him. Yingge's life is legendary and enthusiastic.

Naturally, it has never fallen short of unswerving love which is innocent, tragic, beautiful but sad, melancholy and disappointing! Just as the poem goes, "I have witnessed the pains of parting in the world. However, unexpectedly, when I return, only withered flowers are left...... Youth and blooming flowers can't be retained in the world."

He has manly braveness and the qualities of a gentleman. He has a patriotic heart and sense of responsibility. He doesn't fear violence and difficulties. With both physical and spiritual toiling, he rescued the poor and those who are stricken by disasters. He admires etiquette and rituals, shows respect for the senior and emphasizes filial piety.

In terms of the literary style, the book is simplistic and vivid. It's also feasible to adapt it to a screenplay. Plenty of verbal communications in it are unique. Less stress can be made on opposite figures in it but it's quite successful such as Hu Erpao and Niu Hai.

No doubt, the academician's enthusiastic life is of phenomenal appeal!

Fan Zhengli, Chief Editor, Senior Journalist and Writer of the *Business Times*

April, 2012

Contents

Introduction

At the 16th United Nation's World Productivity League and WAPS Conference held in Antalya of Turkey on November 3, 2010, a 78-year-old academician of Chinese nationality was elected. Among the 15 academicians elected, he's the oldest with the most numerous achievements and most outstanding performances.

The 15 newly elected academicians of different nationalities were extremely excited when they stepped on the red carpet and the podium with the accompaniment of the beautiful and pleasant light music. They deeply knew that WAPS was the greatest science palace led by the United Nations. Hence, they were world-level academicians. How lofty the honor was!

At the brilliantly illuminated lobby rostrum, academician John Heap, chairman of World Productivity League, President Thomas Tuttle of WAPS and academician Chen Shengchang, vice president, awarded the academician certificates and medals to them. Another long standing ovation was heard. At this time, all domestic and foreign academicians happened to hug the old academician of Chinese nationality together and extended their warm congratulations. What kind of charms of his strike a chord with these young and strong domestic and foreign academicians? What makes them full of admiration? It's his old age, his fighting spirit of not giving in to the old age, his phenomenal scientific research achievements, his four scientific corporate management strategies approved as four technological innovations, and his several lasting books which he put a lot of blood to write......

If a man is 78 years old, he should enjoy harmonious family relationships for common people: he should stroll in the park with his grandson, fish beside the river and bask in the sunshine under the eaves...... Ilowever, Yinggc is still likc a warrior who kccps fighting at the frontline of the scientific researches. With numerous battles, struggles and climbs, Yingge had made outstanding contributions to China's science & technology and personnel training. He has made new breakthroughs in high temperature wear-resisting in domestic and foreign metal surface engineering, and made excellent contributions to scientific studies and productivity development. Yingge's pioneering and sacrifice spirits are admirable. In a science test, he climbed onto the 37m rope ladder regardless of his age and risks, reached the top of the power generation boiler and conducted the high temperature metal wear-resisting technology test with plenty of precious data acquired, thus laying a solid foundation for success in future scientific researches. He's a pioneer in domestic high temperature wear and corrosion-resisting field in metal surface projects; besides, he enjoys a great reputation in the world. He has made immense contributions to the transformation and development of China's and even the world's advanced productivity. Hence, he reached the highest palace in the scientific field of the world's productivity development, and won the honorable title of WAPS academician. Yingge has left the glorious academician "footprint" on the red carpet in Turkey.

Just as an ancient Chinese saying goes, men's will does not depend on the number of his age. For Yingge, he's ambitious so he doesn't fear old age. His never-give-up spirit of fighting, struggling and climbing makes people admire him sincerely. He's indeed the model for domestic and foreign academicians to learn from. Not long ago, at the 10th World Conference on Management Science held in Paris, France, Yingge was elected as the vice president of Chinese nationality and won "Best Contribution Award of China's Corporate Management in the World's Management Science". As a result, the Party Committee of Jiaotong University has successively received the letter of congratulations to Mr. Yingge from World Conference on Management Science, China's Management Academic Committee and Academician Committee of China's Productivity Society of WAPS. He won honors and shining glories for Jiaotong University. Comrade Sun Yongchun, former Party Committee Secretary of Jiaotong University, "Academician is a very lofty title. Jiaotong University finally has an academician. It should be congratulated! It means our university has developed and expanded......"

Yingge was easy-going, restrained, low-profiled in conducting himself and never showed off. His glorious performances are still unknown to the world. Liu Yongtai, senior journalist from Global Create Rich medium, said in his interview, "You have obtained the title of WAPS academician which is a rare glory of your life. It's the most glorious event of your life and the glory of Jiaotong University. You should have a good celebration......" He smiled a bit and was lost in deep thoughts. He recalled the past with tears in his eyes, "My fate, my stars, please tell me, why is my life so twisting and arduous? What is on earth burning on the inside? It's enthusiastic blood or the elf of my soul....... I have something that I can't tell in my heart...... I just did something minor for my motherland and won a little glory for my university. I have nothing to say about myself......"

Dear friends, you must want to know an old man could actually make such glorious achievements in his late years. Such unknown efforts and uplifting struggles, his sense of responsibility for his career, his esteem, his courage, his selflessness, his uttermost efforts..... What kind of strength makes him so strong?

At the 16th international heat spray technology seminar in 2003, Professor Allen Read, chairman of International Spray Association and academician of Canadian Academy of Sciences, and Professor Bell, academician of British Royal Academy of Sciences, spoken highly of Yingge's scientific research achievements, "Your scientific research achievements opened up a new field for metal high temperature and wear-resisting, and the application of constant temperature spray under high temperature in the world. Besides, new enlightenment was provided. It's quite valuable......" It's not only a great evaluation of Yingge's "enthusiastic life" and his "ambition" of transcending himself but also an appreciation of Chinese scientists' unremitting efforts in the field. He won glories for Chinese people.

Yingge felt a lot more pressure after being elected as the academician. Should he just stop and enjoy his late years? Or should he keep fighting, struggling and climbing for his enthusiastic life? The image of Paul • Korchagin kept flashing before his eyes. Yingge decides to act like Paul • Korchagin. As long as he lives for one day, he will keep fighting to make greater contributions to the country, society and people, and win glories for his university. According to Yingge, as long as he's alive for one day, he should work hard, live a splendid day, struggle, fight and climb for one day.

He was a kid born in a poor rural family and didn't have the conditions for climbing science peaks. He has passed many tortuous and dangerous paths, climbed many terrible cliffs and experienced many hard times...... Before in the virgin forest of Northeast China, he drove the train, transported the wood and fought against wild wolves, wild boars and tigers, and almost lost his life there. His classmates and comrades-in-arms were buried on that black land. Every time when he went to visit their tombs, he would be extremely sad...... Little did he think he could survive.

Every time when he recalls the dynamic and vigorous scenes during his teaching and scientific research course in the past, Yingge gets carried away. However, in the past decades, his road has been filled with vicissitudes. He has experienced lots of rugged ones. He always thinks he's lucky to survive. He's very contented. He finally reaches the academician height and has left the academician "footprint", which he didn't occur to him before.

Yingge has experienced rough and bumpy roads. Each of his "footprints" carries a legendary story which makes people meditate and find it hard to forget...... His great spirit of fighting, struggling and climbing is quite worth everyone's learning. How should people spend their life? How to complete the trips? What kind of footprints one should leave? It's believed that Yingge's "footprints" will undoubtedly encourage, spur and educate the younger generation, and provide useful enlightenment for you.

Yingge often warns himself, "People's lives are precious. Life should be fervent. You can't just lay idle and you should accomplish something. When you are still alive and have opportunities, you should lose no time to contribute to the motherland!" When the journalist asked about his hard courses, he's so moved that he wept...... Everyone wants success. What does success rely on? How to succeed? The answers will be revealed in The Footprints of the Academician. What kind of "footprints" will Yingge leave us? Let's look forward to it......

Part I Childhood with Misery

1. Fujia Village in Childhood

Shandong people were known for their ambition, desire for excelling, courage and determination in action. The land of Qi and Lu kingdoms in history was today's Shandong province. It had a long-standing history with places of interest spread all over and celebrities coming forth. It boasted ancient Chinese saints as well. The hometown of Confucius, Mencius and Mo-tse was Shandong. Shandong was the birthplace of Han Dynasty culture and dragon culture as well as the cradle of Chinese nation. Stories of the outlaw heroes in Water Margin happened in Shandong. Mount Thai, first of the five mountains in China, was situated in Shandong. The mother river of Chinese nation--the Yellow River converged into Bohai Sea in Shandong. Yingge was born in Fujia Village, a little village in Zhangshe Town, Pingdu city, Shandong, in May 4, 1933. He carried the blood of Shandong people. The family name of all the people in this village was Fu. There's no other family name. About a hundred households lived in this village and they shared such spirits of "poor but ambitious, dauntless and energetic". It's because of such spirits that Fujia village became famous 4,000 meters or 5,000 meters around. In winter, all villagers, be them men or women, old or young, went to the streets and bask in the sun while sitting along the wall. It's because they were so poor that they didn't have firewood to burn and heat their bed. Their houses were humid and wind would blow through cracks on the wall. The water in the urn was an entire piece of ice. Therefore, they'd rather feel warmth under the sun. They talked and gossiped about all things including ancient and modern topics. In this way, they laughed their coldness off.

One day, little Yingge, closely followed by Uncle Haoke, came to join in the fun.

Little Yingge pointed at Uncle, "Look, what's on Uncle's face?" Everybody looked and it turned out that oil was all over Uncle Haoke's face and mouth. Uncle Haoke was a talkative and tough guy who was brave to act and feared nothing.

Therefore, somebody asked "Haoke, why so many oil on your face? Did you eat something good?" Haoke answered with inadvertence, "You said I was broke, didn't you? I had two pig's feet at home today. It's really delicious. Did you have money to buy that?"

The other person doubted, "You are just bragging. You are so poor to put guinea grass on your bed. A family of seven use three quilts and one mattress. Besides, you have four or five kids to raise."

Another person chipped in, "Nobody in our village raise pigs. Even a pig hair can't be seen in your house. How come you have pig's feet to eat?" Everybody laughed out loudly.

Yingge revealed the truth, "He didn't eat pig's feet at all. He just smeared the lamp oil at home onto his mouth and face." Hearing this, people giggled again. Haoke was embarrassed, "You little kid, watch your mouth!"

Some people said Haoke liked bragging and doing something beyond his means. He never admitted his poverty no matter how. He served as the party branch secretary of the village. He led people to work hard in the hope of making poor Fujia village really rich and abundant.

One late autumn, a contest was held among different villages. Tough guys were selected to compete for "plowing and energy". All teams were ready. People who were there to watch the contest wore cotton-padded jackets and trousers. Even so, they still felt cold. However, contestants from Fujia village were bare in the top and didn't fear the coldness at all. With the order set, all teams started working to see which team was the fastest and plowed the greatest length. In the end, Fujia village took the first place and since then, men of Fujia village had been known for their energy and enthusiasm while Fujia village for poor but ambitious, dauntless and energetic spirits. Hence, people in other villages liked to hire people of Fujia village to work for them.

2. On the Way of Fleeing

Fujia Village had three problems in old society: too many long-term migrant workers; small land, great disaster and many beggars; too many people who were drive into a corner and chose to run away from famine. Yingge was faced with the third problem. His family left their hometown in order to escape disasters and famine so he left Fujia Village.

In the extremely evil old society, Yingge had been brought up amid hunger and coldness. Yingge was the fourth child of the family and his three elder brothers went outside for a living in their teens. In an evening of autumn rain of 1940, in order to prevent from being seized to serve as slave laborers and soldiers in the war, seven-year-old little Yingge which, together with his parents, left his hometown and stepped on the way of fleeing from famine and disasters. Yingge's father walked ahead with the carrying pole on his shoulders and Yingge's mother led little Yingge by hand. The three of them walked and teetered on the muddy rural path. Little Yingge pulled his mother's clothes and was followed by his little companion-- a little black dog named Harley.

His mother turned around and said to Yingge, "My kid, dogs are not allowed in the ship and train. Japanese people will kill our dog if they find it. Let's just let the dog go back." Yingge pleaded, "Harley can't leave me and I can't part with Harley, either." Yingge was so sad that he held it in his arms. He kissed Harley and caressed it with his hands. However, mother's words made sense. Little Yingge was so depressed and said while weeping, "Harley, sorry. There's nothing I could do. Go home. We have to part here." He took out a baked roll from his pocket and gave it to Harley. Little Harley swallowed it up quickly due to hunger. Yingge said, "Harley, bye. My baby!" Yingge watched Harley leaving. Harley was quite obedient to Yingge. It kept turning around on the way back with tears in its eyes. Yingge also kept looking over his shoulders while moving ahead with his mother until Harley couldn't be seen anymore. His mother persuaded, "Don't be sad, Yingge. We can't help it. We even don't know our future." Later on, Yingge heard that little Harley returned home and didn't leave until it died of hunger. A neighbor felt pity about it and wanted to take it away but the dog just didn't move. It didn't eat either. The tears in its eyes showed that it's missing Yingge. Tears coursed down Yingge's cheeks whenever he thought of little black dog-- Harley.

Yingge's family passed two port cities Qingdao and Dalian on their way. They reached Dalian port after spending a few days in the sailing ship on the sea. Eventually they came to the famous northern city Harbin after going through all kinds of hardships. What's heard and seen on the way was chilling and shocking. Swaggering Japanese people, with sabers around their waists, rods in hand and wolfhounds beside them, forced Chinese laborers to toil for them at stations and ports such as carrying bean cakes and bags. Chinese people who suffered hunger and cold slaved for Japanese people under the threat of their bayonets. Yingge saw that at the port with ships to be unloaded, a dry-boned laborer with a big bag on his shoulder, suddenly fell onto the ground due to the heaviness on his shoulder and the grains in the bags were scattered all around. A Japanese soldier was indignant and kicked the laborer on the ground for several times. Then two other soldiers came to carry the laborer and threw him into the sea. Therefore, laborers had a strike to show resistance. Only at this time Japanese soldiers were seized with a panic. All these tragic scenes full of blood were deeply engraved on the innocent mind of little Yingge who bore hatred against cruel Japanese soldiers.

With dark night and endless road, the little rural path was marked by the "footprints" of Yingge in his childhood when he fled from disasters.

3. Smart and Brave Little Yingge

Misfortunes never came alone. In 1940, Harbin was the territory of Japanese people and it's hard for poor people to survive. Yingge's second elder brother worked for Japanese people and his scanty salary could barely support himself. What should they do when three more people suddenly came? In particular, in winter, the wind was bitter cold and water became ice. The temperature was as low as minus 45°C～50°C. At that time, Yingge's family lived in a rented idle cowshed in the cattle farm of Russian immigrants. The courtyard was stacked with dry hay for cattle and cow dung. The environment was extremely lousy. Little Yingge had to carry a bag and pick coal cinder everywhere so that his family could get heated with it. In the evening, he carried his cigarette box to sell cigarettes along the streets. One time, a Japanese soldier bullied him and walked away after taking two packets of expensive cigarettes without paying him. Little Yingge caught up with him and asked for money. The soldier refused and even slapped him to the ground. Little Yingge stood up and angrily bite the soldier's hand which was holding the cigarettes. The soldier cried with pains and dragged him to Japanese Military Police while beating him. He locked him in a room of the Military Police. The soldier went to the hospital to see doctor. Before he came back, another officer came in and asked, "You little kid, what are you doing here?" "Your man grabbed my cigarette and I am here to take back my money!" The officer felt undignified to tangle with a kid and ordered, "Get out of here! Otherwise, I will kill you!" A Chinese laborer who was locked in a dark room reminded little Yingge, "You can't get a penny from these robbers. You'd better leave here as soon as possible since the injured soldier hasn't come back. Otherwise, you will be beat hard. Run!" Hearing this, smart Yingge left the devil place and finally kept his life.

It's terribly cold in the northern ice city Harbin. It's thick ice on the outside and white frosts on the inside. Little Yingge's family had no firewood and coal to warm themselves, and shivered with coldness. The eight-year-old little Yingge saw four carts on the street were fully loaded with firewood which was fastened by ropes so he approached it and watched carefully to check how the ropes were fastened and where the joints were. Yingge was so clever to get everything clear soon. Out of a sudden, a Japanese soldier beat little Yingge's face with a big whip. It hurt so much that Yingge cried with hands around his head. A trace of blood print showed up on his face immediately. Next, little Yingge left the carts and vowed to revenge. Therefore, he brought all poor children who picked coal cinder together and worked out a plan of revenge. When those four Japanese soldiers were eating and drinking in the restaurant, little Yingge walked close the carts, took out the knife from his waist and cut the ropes while nobody saw him. He pushed the carts and then stabbed the horse's ass hard with his knife. The alarmed horse ran about wildly and the firewood was scattered all over. Poor children swarmed to pick up the firewood on the ground. The smart Yingge thought to himself: I will wait first. When those Japanese soldiers go chasing the carts, I will take the firewood home.

Hearing the sound of horses and carts, Japanese soldiers had no mood to eat and drink. They rushed outside and were furious to see the scattered firewood. They fired two shots towards the sky before going after the carts. Being frightened by the gun sound, horses ran faster...... It was a chaos on the street. Quite a few trolleys, tricycles and stalls were bumped...... Along the street, pedestrians ran around here and there in order to shun from the running horses. Finally he picked lots of firewood and went home, triumphant with head held high.

Japanese soldiers bullied and oppressed Chinese people and even their children took advantage of that to insult Chinese children. One time, Yingge picked up half bag of coal cinder from

the garbage heap in the courtyard of Japanese soldiers. On his way home, a Japanese kid who were a bit elder than Yingge seized the bag from Yingge, dumped the coal cinder onto the ground and trampled it. Little Yingge got angry, picked a big coal cinder, threw it onto the Japanese kid's face hard and then kicked him. The little Japanese kid felt so painful that he cried and ran home to report to his father. Therefore, his father ran downstairs with his bayonet and tried to arrest Yingge. Yingge felt something was wrong so he jumped from the wall. He ran towards the railway and the kid's father went after him closely. At this time, a train was going to approach with loud whistles. In a twinkling, little Yingge went to the most extreme lengths to cross the rail and right next, the train roared past. It's a narrow escape. Little Yingge was almost run over by the train. The train driver was so scared that he abused: You little bastard! Damn it! The train separated little Yingge and the kid's father. After the train passed and the kid's father tried to catch Yingge, little Yingge had been out of his reach. Yingge hid in a dairy cow lair of a Russian immigrant family. The kid's father looked around in the dark and stinky lair. Hc found nothing and went outside the courtyard. Clever little Yingge picked an ice and threw it onto the main gate.

Hearing the sound, the kid's father thought little Yingge escaped from the main gate so he ran towards that way. Hence, little Yingge fled through the back wall of the lair. Before long, the kid's father came back with a flashlight. He searched the entire lair but didn't see Yingge. He asked the old Russian woman whether she saw a little Chinese kid or not. The old woman shook her head and said no. He slapped her to the ground and then walked away. All this was witnessed by little Yingge who was hiding beyond the wall. He climbed the wall, pulled the old woman up from the ground and helped her walk into the room because it's extremely cold outside and the old woman would be frozen that way.

Little Yingge was afraid that the Japanese father would come back again so he hide in another dairy cow lair. He didn't go home until it's getting dark. His family was badly anxious and tried to find him everywhere. Yingge told the entire story after he went home. His father was timid and afraid of big trouble so he intended to spank him. Yingge's mother wept and stopped him, "He did this because we had no money to buy firewood and coal. Beat me if you want!" After finishing her words, she pulled little Yingge near her and protected him. She said something and cried with sadness while touching the kid's little cold hands. The younger sister of little Yingge sobbed with her mother as well......

Yingge's parents knew that their kid made a big trouble and those ferocious Japanese people wouldn't give up. They would beat little Yingge to death if they got him.

Little Yingge fought a battle of wits and courage with Japanese soldiers in order to survive and prevent his entire family from suffering coldness. Young little Yingge possessed the untamed nature of being smart, brave and unwilling to give in as well as invincible spirits of fearing nothing.

Since then, little Yingge had left the "footprints" of fighting against Japanese soldiers with smartness.

3. Call of Life

Since Yingge beat the Japanese kid, which was a big trouble, the entire family had been restless. Who dared to piss off Japanese people in the era when they dominated the world? Moreover, little Yingge was so audacious in the extreme that he beat a Japanese boy. That's a way to death, wasn't that?! Yingge's father was anxious and desperate so he went to a Shandong fellow-townsman for ideas.

The family name of the fellow-townsman was Fu, too. Yingge called him Brother Fu. He said, "We can't let Japanese people arrest Yingge. Since we can't confront them directly, we can hide. Of the Thirty-Six Stratagems, fleeing is best. Tomorrow I will take Uncle and Yingge to stay for a few days in the village north of the Songhua River. We will see what to do after sizing up the situation."

Yingge's father continued, "There's nothing to eat at home. We will buy some maize meal there and take it back. Yingge's mother and younger sister have nothing to cook. It's really hard to survive in such era when we can feed ourselves for one meal but may have nothing to eat for the next."

The three of them walked on the frozen surface of the Songhua River and headed towards the village north of the Songhua River with the chilly winter wind blowing. After marching for an entire day, they arrived at the house of the fellow-townsman in the village. Few years ago, they fled from their hometown Shandong and came to Heilongjiang province so they felt cordial after seeing each other and would like to care and help each other. After living for a few days here, Yingge and his father found nothing happened so they bought some maize meals and brought them back to their home in Harbin.

The three of them walked along the riverside on the way home with food on their back. It was a night with bright moon shining in the sky. The moonlight illuminated the ice snow on the river surface and it's a vast whiteness. They teetered on the river surface. When they came to the middle of the river, suddenly Japanese soldiers shouted from the riverside, "Stop!" and ran towards them. At that time, Japanese soldiers were seizing economic criminals. The so-called economic criminals referred to urban people who went to villages to buy food. It's a crime imposed on Chinese people by Japanese soldiers. Those who were caught would be beat cruelly and sent to prison.

Regardless of the shouts of Japanese soldiers, they just ran towards home. Those soldiers shot their guns while shouting. They thought: they just couldn't be arrested by those soldiers no matter how! They kept running on the way. It's slippery on the ice snow-covered river surface so they would constantly fall onto the surface while running.

Yingge's father suffered from trachitis. His asthma broke out whenever it's getting cold in winter, especially when it's accompanied by strong wind and snow. The maize meals on his back made him out of breath. Soon he was exhausted and collapsed. He said, "I couldn't walk anymore. You two run first! You must go back alive!" Then he pointed at his fellow-townsman, "I am sorry to bother you. Please help my family! Our children won't forget you when they grow up. Thank you. Please take my kid home! He has suffered enough and should be kept alive! I really can't run and don't want to drag you. Run, please!"

His fellow-townsman replied, "Uncle, we can't leave you here. Stand up. Let's go back together! Come onto my back. Have Yingge carry your food and I will have mine hang from my neck......"

Yingge kneed down beside his father and cried, "Dad, you can't die! Japanese soldiers were coming. If you were arrested and sent to prison, you will be beaten to death. My mother is still waiting for us at home. My younger sister can't die of hunger and coldness! Dad, come on! I will have to go back to pick coal cinder for heating. Dad! Let's go!" Yingge shouted and cried while pulling his father up. Brother Fu carried Yingge's father on his back. The wind on the river surface was blowing hard. They were walking with difficulty. Suddenly, they slipped and both of them fell onto the ground. They had to stop and have a rest, having no strength at all to move.

Suddenly, those Japanese soldiers who were after them disappeared. No shouts could be heard anymore and not a soul could be seen. Where were they? It turned out that they were just focusing on chasing them under the moonlight and didn't notice the ice holes on the river surface which were dug by fishermen in the day to capture fish with nets. Those Japanese soldiers dropped into the ice hole and were washed away by the water. Just as the old saying went, wickedness does not go altogether unrequited!

On the river surface, the three of them had a break for a while under the moonlight and the starry sky. Then they continued their journey. Brother Fu had Yingge's father on his back and walked slowly. Yingge followed them with food bags on his back.

The dark night passed and day broke. They eventually got home! Yingge's mother cried with joy seeing the three of them returned safe. She held the thigh of Yingge's father and sobbed, "Finally you come back. I have been so terrified. I thought you will never come back. Now everything is solved!" Little Yingge wept as well and the entire family were so glad that they wept about their reunion.

Yingge's mother said, "Two Japanese soldiers came to look for Yingge after you left. They asked in blunt Chinese, 'Did you see the child who beat our Japanese kid?' They left after seeing no kid in the house. It's really dangerous! Yingge was lucky. If he stayed at home, he would have been taken away and beaten to death! Our kid is really lucky!" Yingge's mother embraced Yingge in her arms and burst into a rage of tears, "Good boy! You are really blessed......!" They didn't stay there for long after coming back. They were afraid that Japanese soldiers would return to seize little Yingge. They wouldn't just give up like that. Later on,

Yingge's family fled to the village north of the Songhua River where they settled and farmed with their fellow-townsman.

Little Yingge had grown up in such environment full of hardships and difficulties. Life was encouraging and calling him to work harder and live with courage......

At that time, little Yingge herded pigs and horses for others in the day, and learned "Three Character Classic" from an old teacher of the village in the night. He lived for four years in the village. His family didn't move back to Harbin until 1945 when Harbin was recovered and Japanese soldiers surrendered.

12-year-old Yingge thought he had "come of age". He had left the "footprints" of calling of life and continued survival on the black land of the village.

5. Change of Destiny

Little Yingge sat at the kerbside of the street. While looking up at the sky, he was thinking, expecting and humming:

My destiny, my stars, do you know? You tell me;

Why does life tease me in such a cruel way,

Why am I so poor that I suffer from hunger and coldness,

I run about here and there for exploration,

Oh, destiny, Ah, Ah......

Why are other people rich and why do they have fur coat in winter and shirt in summer to wear,

Destiny, my stars,

I am so skinny and have to worry about food and clothes all days,

Other people are so rich that they are fat with radiance shining on their faces,

Oh, destiny, where is my bright future? How should I move on the road?

Yingge fantasied all the time: I want to be rich. I refuse to give in. I want to get rid of poverty. My destiny, oh, my destiny. I don't rely on God nor I depend on something else. I will go to work and pull carts. I want to earn money and I will be rich. I want to go to school, achieve something and get somewhere. Oh, destiny......Ah...... Yingge sat at the kerbside and was singing in a low voice.

One day, Yingge was walking outside and saw a group of poor people pulling and pushing carts with strenuous efforts on a big slope. They were acting as slowly as snails. Some kids helped push the carts while shouting “Whoops”. Yingge went towards the front of another cart, “Uncle, can I help you?”

The cart pusher: “Good, very good. I will pay you if you help me pull it up the slope.”

Yingge took out the rope and fastened it onto the little cart. He spared no effort to help pull the cart and finally succeeded. In the end, the cart pusher gave him five cents.

That person said to him amiably, “You worked really hard. Come to work for me here every day. Cart pulling can earn you a lot of money.”

Since then, Yingge had found a way of earning money and the direction of his life. As long as he earned money, he could go to school and study in college. With knowledge and abilities, he could change his destiny, have food to eat and survive in the world...... Eventually he could support his family.

Whenever it’s about dusk every day, he would go to a private supplementary school. He stood outside the classroom. He’s short so he stood on two piled bricks beside the window. He listened to the teacher there and wrote down what the teacher lectured under the light. Besides, he followed the teacher to re-read the lectured contents.

After class and during the break, Yingge sat on a step of the stairs to solve maths problems and memorize what the teacher had taught......

One of those little students playing in the courtyard was naughty and tough. He came to sneer at Yingge, “You poor wretch. You actually stealthily listened to our teacher without paying tuition.” He snatched Yingge’s notebook and threw it onto the ground.

Yingge was furious and became wild, “Damn you. You dare to bully me.”

The student glared at him, “I am abusing you. So what? Beat me?”

Being enraged, Yingge went forward to hold him and wanted to throw him down. However, the student was taller and stronger than Yingge. The two of them got into a fight. Quite a few pupils came to watch and shouted "Come on!". In an instance, the student threw Yingge onto the ground.

Yingge stood on his feet. He was ambitious although he was small. He didn't show weakness and rushed to him again after smearing his mouth. Some people were shouting "Come on!" constantly. Yingge was quite smart and adopted the strategy of "lure the enemy away from his base". He pointed behind his back, "Look, someone is coming to beat you......" At this time, Yingge took the advantage to slapped him hard and kicked his penis with his foot. The student lay on his stomach with hands covering his crotch. He kept crying and shouting on the ground due to great pain!

Hearing the chaos, a teacher came out and yelled, "Why do you fight with each other?" A group of students pointed towards Yingge...... Yingge told the whole story and the teacher learned about the reason. He hurried to check the student on the ground and massaged his crotch. After a while, the student stood up. The teacher said, "Get into the classroom! Don't fight anymore in future!"

The teacher turned to Yingge, "Well, you can sit in the classroom as well and in the back row."

Yingge said, "Thank you, teacher, but I can't go inside. I may as well stay beside the window."

The teacher was wondering, "Why not?" Yingge lowered his head and felt embarrassed......

Yingge answered, "I am poor and I didn't pay tuition. I will sit in the classroom when I earn enough money."

The teacher was so moved, "You are a thoughtful kid. It's okay. You can go inside and I won't ask for money from you."

Class began and the teacher talked to everyone in an education manner, "My students, you are not allowed to bully little

Yingge anymore. You need to help the poor. He's very ambitious and ideal. He wants to study because he desires to change his destiny of poverty. Knowledge is power. Knowledge is money. Only when you have knowledge can you do something great and get somewhere. With knowledge, you can change your destiny."

"Little Yingge, although he's small, he's uplifting and aspiring. He wants to go through primary school, middle school and even college. You need to regard him as an example. He is indomitable and diligent with a great ambition......"

After class, the teacher called Yingge and gave him two books, a notebook and two pencils, "Go review what we have learned today and come tomorrow." Then he took out two baked rolls from his bag and handed them to Yingge, "It's too late and you must be hungry. Take them."

What an amiable and loving teacher. Yingge bore what happened today on his mind forever and was determined to study hard in future and repay the teacher in future.

Yingge was so touched that he kneed down in front of the teacher to extend his respect and gratitude. The teacher helped him up quickly, "It's all right. Don't mention it." With tears on his cheeks, he stood up. The teacher hugged him and wept as well...... For a long while, the two of them couldn't speak a word. Yingge told what happened in the school to his mother after going home, and gave the baked rolls to his mother and younger sister, "I already ate one." Actually he just wanted to save them for his family...... He went to bed with hunger.

Yingge was eager to be the first so he worked hard and spared no effort to earn money. He had a goal on mind-- cart pulling. Since then, he could earn money to pay tuition and go to school with self-assurance. Every day he tried to get the first rope to pull. He's too tired and had little food to eat. Besides, he did a lot of work. Therefore, he suddenly lay on his stomach due to the slippery ground. The cart pushers couldn't stand. The cart and Yingge rolled along the big slope. The cart which carried so many cargo glided fast on the slope. Yingge slided under the little cart and it's so dangerous that he was almost killed by the heavy cart. His knees scraped and his face bleed. The cart pusher gave him one jiao immediately and asked him to see doctor. Yingge ignored the pain and directly went home with money. Seeing the blood on his face and legs, his mother hugged Yingge and cried, "It's too dangerous to pull carts outside. Don't go there anymore. You are too young." Yingge refused, "Mum, I will still go pulling carts because I want to earn money and go to school. The teacher said that only knowledge can change our destiny of poverty."

That's Yingge. He went through hardships year after year in order to pursue knowledge and make a living. He was never defeated and never feared difficulties. After completing primary courses in the private school, he studied again after passing the examination of public primary school which didn't ask for tuition.

After graduating from the primary school, Yingge could write and calculate, and thought he's a grown-up already. He believed that he became a well-educated man and had grasped so much knowledge that the entire Harbin city couldn't accommodate anymore. The little river couldn't raise the big fish anymore. He held his head high and back straight when walking on the streets. It seemed that everything was a piece of cake for him. There's nothing he couldn't deal with. With knowledge, he could do great things and make a fortune.

One day, he asked his two classmates, his best companions--Liang Yunchao and Yang Anguo to go to the streets and look for jobs which required well-educated men, thus earning more money to support families.

The three of them came to Harbin Institute of Railway in Nangang District of Harbin which was the highest institution of higher learning of the Ministry of Railways. With an air of "arrogance", they entered the office building paved with red carpets. It's the first time Yingge saw the red carpet so he touched it with his hand. He was envious, "How clean it is!" He took off his shattered rubber shoes immediately and rubbed them against his clothes so as not to make the red carpet dirty. They came to the principal office. The secretary asked, "Who are you looking for, little friends?" Yingge answered, "Someone who's in charge of the entire building." The secretary asked again, "Can you be more specific?" "The first and greatest of your building, the one who has the say."

The secretary replied, "Then you must be looking for the principal. He's the number one here. His words count." The secretary introduced the principal.

The principal asked, "Little friends, what are you here for? Is there anything important?"

Yingge rushed to say, "Do you need educated men here?"

The principal continued, "How well are the three of you educated? What strengths do you have?"

Yingge answered, "We graduated from Northeast Primary School. We passed examinations. We have learned a lot and know a lot. We can write and calculate. Besides, we can do heavy work and without complaining about tiredness......"

The principal laughed loudly and bend forward and backward to hear that, "Little friends, I don't think we can hire great talents like you who graduate from primary school. Sanitation workers here graduate from middle school at least..... What we need are college students instead of primary school and middle school students. You need to go to college if you want to do something great and become genuinely educated. Do you understand?"

Seeing something was wrong, Liang Yunchao pulled Yingge's clothes immediately, "Let's get out of here. Don't argue."

The three "well-educated men" lowered their heads after walking out of the building. Their dream of doing something great was put a damper on. They felt so down and walked on the street without any aim.

"Let's wait and see! We are bound to become well-educated men in future. They will know how awesome we are." Yingge said with unwillingness to submit while walking.

Yang Anguo also shouted while walking, "It's not that easy to go to college. We haven't finished our middle school. It's not known yet whether we can enter middle school or not. College? We are daydreaming. It's nothing great to complete primary school. Bullshit! Nothing great can be done...... Bullshit! Just bragging!"

Yingge was angry to hear that.

He questioned, "What? You don't want to go to college? Stupid! Come and I will beat you to death." Then he took off one of his broken shoes, uncovered Yang Anguo's clothes and spanked him. Liang Yunchao came to stop him quickly, "Stop it." Yang Anguo shook off and ran away in fear.

Yingge asked again, "Liang Yunchao, do you want to go to college or not? You are stupid too!!"

Liang Yunchao was so scared that he couldn't tell directly, "I, I, I want. I want. Don't spank me!"

The three pupils studied hard for six years with extra tutoring in night school. They successfully completed junior and senior high school. Finally they had been successively admitted to college after different, strenuous and twisting roads and their own legendary stories. Yang Anguo entered Harbin Institute of Technology, Liang Yunchao went to Harbin Medical University and Yingge was admitted to Heilongjiang University. They had their dreams come true. They became genuine college students and well-educated men. Later on, Yang Anguo worked as a researcher in National Metal Institute, Liang Yunchao became the director of Harbin Medical University Hospital and Yingge had the honor to be elected as the academician of WAPS.

The three poor kids became great experts in reality after completing their fantasy college life. Their ambitions were fulfilled and they presented their scientific achievements on the stage of international sciences. They shouted: Look. Are you envious! Are you jealous! We are great Chinese people. Let them say "You are not good at anything!" Actually we can do everything!

The road of pursuing dreams is tortuous and it's marked with Yingge's "footprints" of seeking schooling and knowledge.

Part II Snowy Forest

1. Passionate Youth Period in Virgin Forest

With independence, Yingge completed his study in private primary school and middle school while working for others to earn tuition. Later, he was admitted to Northeast Forest Industry Technical College with excellent performance and studied locomotive power under the free supply system. He graduated in autumn of 1951 after three years of hard working when the war to resist U.S. aggression and aid Korea was fought. The frontline of Korea was in badly need of yeddo spruce wood in northeast provinces for repairing roads and trenches, and building bridges. The central government starved for developing the forest resources in the northeast virgin forest so over a hundred technical and secondary school graduates in Harbin were chosen to work in the forest. They left their alma mater and headed for Heilongjiang Dahai Forestry Bureau. These hot-blooded youngsters sang the song of the voluntary army and the youth league……: "Goodbye, my father! My mother! Don't be sad. Don't be depressed. Just wish us a good trip!" Just like soldiers going out to battle, they forged ahead enthusiastically to the place where they were needed most with their heads held high. Yingge and his classmates sang the song of farewell happily while leaving for the remote frontier-- the Snowy Forest.

Get on! Go to fight in the battlefield.
The siren blows. I am singing my song.
Both happiness and hardships will be encountered.
So it's with love and tears.
We have to accept both wine and bitter water.
Both success and death may be waving to you.
Goodbye, my mum. I am leaving you.
Wish your son a good trip!
Good mum! I will always keep you in mind.

Wish me come back to kiss and hug you as early as possible.

Don't be sad. Don't worry about me.

Wish me a nice trip!

Bye, mum. I will miss you.

Bye, mum. Take care of yourself all the time.

I will regularly come back to see you.

In the autumn of 1951, in order to respond to the country's policy, Yingge went to the place where he's mostly needed. He graduated in advance, left his dear mother and his alma mater Northeast Forest Industry Technical College, and headed for remote areas……

He came to the virgin forest of Lesser Khingan Mountains in Mudanjiang River area, the coldest place in China, to safeguard his motherland and participate in the war to resist U.S. aggression and aid Korea, drive the train to deliver wood, and build bridges for transportation. Anyway, it's an era with flames of war raging everywhere.

It's Snowy Forest where the story of the famous hero Yang Zirong fighting against bandits and vulture happened. Different beasts haunted in the virgin forest and often people were swallowed by beasts. Besides, remnant bandits robbed and plundered……

In the compartment, there were eight classmates graduating from the same college with Yingge. The rest of people included literary and art workers of Harbin, girls from the Academy of Finance & Economics and the Institute of Engineering. They were talking and singing happily. Young people were so enthusiastic and they looked forward to beautiful future in the hope of doing something great.

The entire compartment was permeated with youngsters' happy laughters of not knowing what sadness was and their youth vitality.

They sang in unison: Goodbye, father and mother, don't be sad. Wipe off you tears. Don't be depressed. Wish us a good trip!

Goodbye, mother. You son will come back soon to hug and kiss you.

Of course some of them lowered their heads and were thinking about their mothers. These young people who had never left home went out for the first time so it's natural that they hated to part with their mothers.

It's really cold in the Snowy Forest Lesser Khingan Mountains! The temperature outdoor was as low as less than minus 50°C and dripping water froze. Some people were thinking: Could I survive in such bitter cold area? Some people were afraid: it's heard that beasts often hang out there, which sounded really thrilling. In the evening, wild boars might break the door, bit and ate people. If it's so, how could I get back to Harbin and reunite with my mother?

The girl Feng Qinqin (Little Feng) whose major was accounting was a graduate of the Academy of Finance & Economics. Fixing her eyes on Yingge, she wanted to approach him this moment but lowered her head with shyness next moment. It seemed that she wanted to ask Yingge his name but feared to say that directly. Just as the old saying went, it's easy to meet with each other but hard to know each other……

Yingge looked sidelong at her and already knew what's on her mind. He took the first step to go talking, "Hi, girls, let's sing a song……" Yingge sang first, "I have wandered around half of the universe but failed to find my love. I have seen lots of girls but you are the cutest. Your eyes are the brightest. Your body is the hottest. Your eyes are as blue as the sea. They can smile and deliver affection. Let's sing out our love on the inner side. With your love and affection, your fragrance spreads afar…… I will miss you no matter where you go……I will follow you……I won't leave you……Oh, stars, Oh, the moon, you……"

On the way, countless towering trees such as pine trees and poplars stretching towards the sky swept fast on both sides of the rail. The autumn scenery was extremely beautiful. The entire forest was dyed red. Different flowers sent out their fragrance. Green pines and verdant cypresses could be seen everywhere. Colors were rich such as fiery red, ivory white and dark green. It's a profusion of colors….. The train was speeding along. Youngsters were bold and unrestrained. They were singing with elatedness. Soon they reached their destination Dahai Forestry Bureau where Yingge fought. "Don't be sad. Don't be depressed. Wish us a good trip……" The singing could still be heard and the train was still running fast. Soon they arrived at the bureau station.

Since then, Yingge had left the pioneering "footprint" on the boundless Snowy Forest.

2. Unforgettable Passion

Yingge was walking with his classmates on Linhai Avenue towards the Forestry Bureau. They seemed immersed in deep thought: there must be bitterness, sweetness and love here. Only the coexistence of bitterness and sweetness demonstrates true love.

Love represented coexistence of two genders. Neither possessed love fragrance alone forever from night to dawn.

I would sing my song and go my way...... There would be both bitterness and happiness. However, I couldn't stop. I wouldn't turn around if nothing was achieved.

In order to welcome the first batch of graduates and young intellectuals to work in deep mountains and forests, Dahai Forestry Industry Bureau held an entertainment party. It's boisterous and as bright as day at the campfire party.

Director General Yuan made a welcoming speech, "Dear comrades, at this evening of red orange osmanthus and blossoming flowers and on behalf of Dahai Forestry Industry Bureau Party Committee and all employees of the bureau, first allow me to extend my sincere welcome to the new young comrades and college graduates. Welcome to join in the construction in Dahai Forestry Bureau and contribute your talent, wisdom and youth. Your arrival brings us strength and vitality. We would like to extend sincere welcome and gratitude!"

Secretary Sun of the Party Committee made a passionate speech as well, "Dear comrades! Our motherland and people need you so does Dahai Forestry Bureau! The frontline of the war to resist U.S. And aid Korea needs you more! You give up the superior life in the big city and come to the tough deep forests and mountains to contribute your youth and strength to building motherland and developing the virgin forest. Here I would like to extend my respect and gratitude! Today we hold an evening party to welcome your arrival. Let's extend our welcome with happy songs, graceful dances and rich entertainment shows!" Secretary Sun was sent by the Railway Bureau to take charge of Party work.

"Next let's give the floor to Yingge, representative of our young graduates!"

Yingge ascended the rostrum with high spirits.

"Respectful Secretary Sun, Director General Yuan of Forestry Bureau, Factory Director Li, Dear Comrades and friends, Good Evening! We are from different places of the country but we gather in this beautiful land of forests. Here, on behalf of new comers, I feel honored to extend our gratitude to leaders and comrades of the Forestry Bureau. Wish the evening party a success!"

Today is a day which is worth celebrating. We young intellectuals come to the Snowy Forest to develop the virgin forest for our motherland. We feel extremely excited. Today is a day of happiness, elation and commemoration as well!

The autumn wind is cool and the orange osmanthus smells fragrant.

The jade lotus is bright-colored and the autumn chrysanthemum is sweet-smelling.

"We have strong leaders, able workers, young and beautiful girls, young and handsome boys. We are determined to sing along and develop the virgin forest on this black land. We know very well that we will encounter both bitterness and happiness in the process. However, we will hang in there in order to make our motherland bigger and stronger. We will forge ahead without turning back. Thank you!"

Secretary Sun announced that the evening party started.

Where there were young people, there was vitality, hope and happiness.

Yingge stood out in the crowd because of his tall stature, good body shape, big eyes and bushy eyebrows, nose right at the center of the standard face shape, shining eye contacts. He always had his head held high while striding forward. Every move of his sent out the atmosphere of youth and vitality. Besides, he spoke quite standard Putonghua and his voice was always sonorous. Yingge was so handsome.

Yingge was not only the monitor of the school but also the organizer of entertainment activities. He's gifted in this aspect. His dance was beautiful with demeanor and charms of Russian dance as well as sentiment and romance of Paris imperial court dance. He stole the show at the evening party.

The shows at the evening party were varied such as solo, cross talk and dance. The most excellent performance was "Song of Emancipation" sung by Feng Qinqin and her solo dance. Her elegant dance and lark-like singing voice shocked the entire audience. Young boys stared at her in a trance. They were frozen seeing that her coquettish body danced with the happy melody. Her excellent performance won warm applause of the entire audience.

The next show was tenor solo: "My Sun"-- a famous Italian song from Yingge. The entire audience was taken aback by his performance as well.

In the end it's social dance. After having a slow three-step dance, Feng Qinqin and the director general of the bureau sat on the bench to take a break. Her "cool but elegant" and "proud" temperament attracted quite a few young boys to look over their shoulders frequently. Some young boys' heartbeat sped up and faces blushed. They wanted to invite her to a dance but felt shy. Yingge looked at her with affection. They looked into each other's eyes and struck sparkles of love just like lightening. Feng Qinqin stood up and generously invited handsome Yingge for a quick three-step dance. The two of them danced well and cooperated tacitly, thus presenting a beautiful dance. The more they danced, the more enthusiastic. Just as the song was finished, little Ma and Liu Dan of the song and dance ensemble seized the opportunity to invite Yingge for Latin, Cha-cha and Rumba which were more phenomenal and intoxicating. The pursuit of love brought about charming dances which triggered a sensation time and again. It seemed a dance ball. The happy atmosphere at the party was rising. Happiness and passion made the joyful atmosphere almost burst. Some people said this evening was the greatest enjoyment of life. At this moment, people forgot all frustrations and anxiety. It's all about sparkles of love and unforgettable moving scenes as well as soul affection that couldn't be pacified. Who said the Snowy Forest was rustic? Who said there's no happiness here? Who said there were no beautiful girls here? Who dared to say there's no love here? It's a miraculous place. Even if it's dark night, you could still see the light of love. It's quick three-step first, then Latin and then the more difficult Waltz. They kept dancing until only few of them were left to perform, which won intermittent applauses and cheers.

The dance ball was over but young people were reluctant to part. Yingge and amorous girls kept talking like twittering birds. What an awesome dance of the handsome boy! Boys like him were few! At this moment, a girl said to another, "Well? Are you into him? Go for him! Go!" The girl replied, "Who? I think you also like him. You go with him!"

"So what? I m going right now. You can't stop me from liking him!"

People walked out of the party site amid bursts of laughters and returned to their own dorm to silently memorize, thinking and longing...... Who could attract Yingge and win Yingge's love? Yingge was the Prince Charming of all girls.

At the dance ball, Yingge and Feng Qinqin fell in love with each other at the first sight. After spending some time together, the two of them couldn't help each other and Feng Qinqin became Yingge's first girlfriend. Some people said, "There were three kinds of power in the world: political power, economic power and power of love." Love was sweet and it could produce infinite power to overcome difficulties.

Yingge had been brought up amid difficulties so he was soon adapted to the arduous environment of the forestry. Besides, with his sweet girlfriend, he was happy to do anything without feeling like complaining. He worked with diligence and happiness every day so he made fast progress in businesses. Before long he was promoted to Dache (official locomotive driver) and became a technical backbone of the bureau. He's good at using his wits so technical reform was his strength. He paid greater attention to safety production. No accident had ever happened in the trains he drove so soon he was assessed as technical pacesetter and safety pacesetter. Later on, he was promoted to assistant engineer of the driver instructor. In order to enhance the old and new drivers' technical level, he organized training classes to lecture for senior technical personnel. He taught the construction mechanism of the locomotives, dynamics, applied physics and accident handling, etc. He was often praised by superior leaders and technicians, deeply trusted by superior leaders, respected and admired by college graduates.

3. Make Friends with Wild Wolves

Few days later, it's Yingge's turn to drive the train to the logging camp in the mountain area Toudaogou Forest for transporting wood.

The busiest part in the forest was to pile up wood. The felled logs were transported from the mountains and stacked in piles just like hills. In this way, it's easy to load the trains. As the hills were formed, it would get harder and harder to stack. Some logs were as heavy as over two tons and required 12 people to carry one log. One of the 12 people must lead the team by singing a working song to carry the log. It would get dangerous even if one team member was not consistent with the rhythm. They shouted loudly in unison: Hia! Hia! Hia-hia-hia! 12 people made concerted efforts to pile up one log after another, which showed huge strength of teamwork. The heavy piling-up work was taken charge of by young and strong men each of whom needed to bear several hundreds of jin on average. If one was distracted, balance would be lost and there would be two results: logs rolled off the pile or even worse, people may be killed. The construction site was crowded with workers and vehicles. People were working in full swing and piling up logs in order. Suddenly Feng Qinqin came to the site. The young worker Little Ma peeped at beautiful Feng while carrying logs so he missed one step and 12 people fell off the springboard at the same time. The big log rolled for over 50 meters and almost ran over people. Everyone was blaming Little Ma for being absent-minded. Some workers shouted: seeing a beautiful girl, you are at loss, aren't you? Someone tried to beat him. All of a sudden, it's a chaos in the lumber storage yard…… Feng was scared, not knowing what to do.

Yingge was perplexed and came over to ask Feng Qinqin, "What are you doing here?" Feng answered, "I come to see you!"

Yingge said, "Girls are not allowed to watch when workers are piling up logs."

She said, "It's cold. I bring you a sweater."

"You shouldn't come here. It's really dangerous just now……" Yingge blamed.

However, Yingge became grateful immediately, "Thank you so much for your sweater. There's no dorm for girls here. It's getting dark. Let me walk you back. I will be worried if you go back alone. There are lots of wild wolves here."

Feng Qinqin was sent by the bureau to serve as a log statistician and help measure logs.

Yingge and Little Feng went downhill, hand in hand. It took another two days to load all logs so there's still time to walk Feng Qinqin back. After walking for over 100 meters, suddenly a gray male wolf sprang from the dense forest and stood in their way. Instantly they were thrilled and terrified. They were bare-handed so they dared not confront the wolf and turned their direction. The wolf kept standing in their way. They were so horrified. However, the wolf, against its wild nature, wagged its tail like a docile dog and looked at them as if it's begging them.

Clever Yingge noticed from its eyes that the wolf wanted them to go to its den because he knew that wild wolves were intelligent according to his experience. Nonetheless, he didn't know the reason. Maybe it's good or it's bad. It boded ill rather than well! Why did the wolf want them to go to the den?

He said to Feng Qinqin immediately, "We can't just wait here for death. The wolf was abnormal. It's terrible. We can't beat them. I heard that the most horrible thing is that the wolf supported its mouth against the ground to 'bellow' because many other wolves will be called. Then we have no way to live! You go back first! I want you to be alive. I will stay to check what on earth the wolf is up to."

Little Feng said, "Can't you see? The wolf wanted to feed other wolves with you. You can't go. At this time of the year, wild wolves came downhill to hunt for preys and food. I can't leave you!"

"Little Feng! Listen to me. You run first. You have parents and are their only child. I can't see you die. Your parents miss you and can't leave you! If we stay here, none of us can live. You go get someone. Maybe I can be saved." Feng Qinqin cried and kneed down with her hands holding Yingge's thigh, reluctant to leave.

Yingge persuaded her to leave, "Tell my parents that I am sorry that I can't perform my filial duty. They raise me up but I can't let them live a happy life. I am so sad! Let them take care of themselves......" He sobbed, "Bye, little Feng. You run!" Yingge risked his life in order to let Feng Qinqin live. There's no time to think more. At the crucial juncture, Yingge pushed Feng Qinqin away with force.

The wolf walked ahead quietly and kept looking back towards Yingge. Yingge was frightened and carefully followed the wolf. As they passed a hillock, the whining sound of wolves in the mountains were heard. Having its ears on edge, the male wolf jumped out all of a sudden and ran towards the place where the sound came from. Soon Yingge heard people scream and then it's a hush. The male wolf returned to Yingge like an arrow and blood was all over its body.

Yingge was confused and terrified...... The farther they walked, the more horrible Yingge felt. He walked behind the wolf like biting the bullet. They came under a big pine tree and here went a terrible scene. A hunter was lying in a pool of blood. Dark red blood flowed out of his throat. Yingge was so afraid that he almost fell. It's quite normal for the male wolf to bite someone to death. Yingge thought: what if he does that to me? It's wolves' nature to eat people. Yingge had a bee in his head and it seemed that death was calling him. Suddenly, Yingge found that the rear leg of a female wolf was stuck in a clamp beside the tree. Two wolf whelps were staying with their mother and protecting her. Their eyes reflected horrible blue lights. It seemed that they were ready to jump on Yingge and bite him to death at any time......

Behind it was a cave entrance and nobody knew how many wolves there were in the cave. It's a wolf den! At this moment, Yingge understood it all. The male wolf forced him to come here to save the female wolf. The dead hunter wanted to seize his prey and take the female wolf but was bit to death by the male wolf. Yingge was anxious: it's either death or life before him. What if the female wolf bit him to death after he saved her? It's easy for four wolves to swallow him up. As the old saying went: wolves don't have conscience. They were brutal and cold-blooded. There's nothing you could do with them. Wolves were meant to eat people.

Yingge also thought that if he didn't save the female wolf, the male wolf wouldn't let him go and Yingge couldn't live. Yingge hesitated again: One good turn deserves another. Yingge tried to step back and approach the clamp but the female wolf cried, which almost made Yingge's heartbeat stop. Yingge was afraid to go forward. The male wolf pressed her head with his head and said something. The female wolf laid down. The male wolf howled towards Yingge and seemed to say, "Please do it!" Yingge decided to try and grit his teeth to go up. He pedaled the clamp to let go the female wolf which was saved and stood up. The female wolf licked the blood on her legs, looked at Yingge and then the male wolf. With the two young wolves, the female wolf hobbled into the mountains while keeping looking back as if she's trying to extend her "gratitude". Yingge finally exhaled.

The male wolf wagged his tail and stared at Yingge with his gentle eyes. It seemed that he didn't want to eat Yingge at all. Yingge trembled. The male wolf lied on his stomach and looked at Yingge with his tail wagged as if he was grateful to the "benefactor" for saving the female wolf. Yingge had a sigh of relief at this time. He could stay alive because the male wolf didn't act. It's better to leave this dangerous place!

The sun set. The forest at twilight appeared especially gruesome and horrible. Yingge's hairs stood on end. He went back along the way he came. He mustered up his courage to check how the male wolf responded. The male wolf sat, motionless, and saw Yingge off the mountains. Yingge sped up but not far away showed up another two gray wolves. He was terrified with cold sweats and thought to himself: Oh, damn it. I was going to die this time. Here came two gray wolves after escaping from the male wolf. The two wolves rushed towards him. He was at a loss and his legs gave way. Suddenly the male wolf came to his rescue. In a twinkling, the male wolf sprang over one of the gray wolves and ripped off one ear. Next he beat another wolf. Bodies were blown to pieces and it's a chaos. A life-death struggle was started. As Yingge tried to run, a gray wolf came for him. The male wolf seized the gray wolf and bit it so Yingge escaped. At this time, lights of torches were seen and sounds of drums and gongs were heard in the east. Little Feng came with other people to save Yingge.

Yingge finally relaxed. This time real saviors came. Hearing the sound, and seeing the flames, the three wolves ran away. Ill luck was turned into good one. The lovers hugged each other and cried. Little Feng talked and cried. She kneed down to hold Yingge's thigh this moment and next stood up to hug Yingge.

"My savior! It's you who saved me from danger. It's hard to imagine you are still alive. I thought we would never see each other. How did you escape from the wolf? How come...... Oh, my God! The wolve didn't eat you." Feng Qinqin cried hard, "Thanks God! How did you escape from the wolf den? How did you stay alive? Tell me! My love, it's a miracle. You are alive. I was so scared. From now on we will be good and we will never part with each other." They embraced each other and cried. People present were moved and tears coursed down their cheeks.

This ordinary young man--Yingge gave away the life opportunity to his girlfriend and left death to himself while being confronted with the life-death test. This was the loftiest and most rare gift as well as the most precious love in the world.

In the Snowy Forest with unforgettable memories, Yingge had left the "footprints" of fighting against and escaping from the wolf den with his braveness and wisdom.

4. The One Who Escaped from Wild Boar Forest

In the earlier autumn, everyone was busy in loading the train with wood which was to be transported to the lumber storage yard of the forestry bureau. It's not Yingge's turn to drive the train. He's supposed to take charge of the 208 train the day after tomorrow. The director general ordered, "The 205 train is used for both passenger and freight transportation. The central chief which came to the forest area to inspect work, the military representative who examined the wood quality and leaders of the railway department will take the train. The bureau leaders pay great attention to the task and especially stresses that a driver who is politically reliable and proficient in driving must be chosen to perform this special task. The one who drives the train shoulders great responsibilities. Should any accident occur, the safety of the chief will be directly endangered. Therefore, safety is the first and foremost priority!" After common discussion of the locomotive depot and the forestry bureau leaders, the driving task was assigned to the assistant engineer Dache Yingge.

Yingge was entrusted to drive the 205 train at a critical moment. He's worried because the lives of over 200 people were in his hand! He couldn't make any mistake. In order not to let down the bureau leaders, Yingge accepted the arduous ask with pleasure and braveness. First he examined the electromechanical equipment and mobile machinery of the train, and then repeatedly checked the braking device. The train was in good status. The assistant driver, the stoker and he held a driving mobilization meeting: "Everyone should perform his own duties, regard the chief's safety as the priority and smoothly complete the important task assigned by the forestry bureau. The three of us must guarantee safe driving with our life! We must bear it on mind!"

After everything was ready, the 205 train set out on time. The train was running safely on the rail in the mountains. Everything was normal. Not far away was Wild Boar Ridge below which was Big Sea Wave River. The water was deep and waves were strong. It's the only way which must be passed by wild wolves, wild boars, tigers and leopards. It's the place where animals drank water so many accidents happened here. In order to ensure absolute safety of the chief, passengers and national property, superior leaders ordered not to stop at Wild Boar Ridge because casualties were caused before when the train stopped here for repair. Just as the train arrived at Wild Boar Ridge, the assistant driver shouted suddenly, "Watch out! A person ahead!" A person laid down on the rail ahead. At the critical moment, the right decision must be made. Should they keep driving or stop to save the person? There's no time to hesitate. Yingge decisively chose the latter. The assistant driver implored, "We can't stop here! The locomotive depot ordered that the train can't be stopped. There are special signals at different stations. It's a special train which not only carry wood but also have three passenger compartments where the central, provincial and bureau leaders who come to examine work sit. Therefore, absolute safety is required. Green lights are turned on at all stations. It's a non-stop train. If it stops, the entire section will be affected and the general deployment will be disrupted. All trains will be late. We must think about the consequences. It's an order from superior leaders! We have to follow it! We will be severely punished by superior leaders if we stop here."

Yingge couldn't think too much. He couldn't just see the person die! His conscience motivated him to brake immediately. Yingge got off the train and it turned out that it's an old Korean aunt beside whom was a basket of mushrooms. Her left leg was bit by the serpent while picking mushrooms in the mountains and swelled a lot. It's dark purple and her life was endangered. There's no time to lose; otherwise the poison would run all over her body. At that time, nobody could save her. Without hesitation, Yingge took out a knife from his waist and stabbed the swelling thigh of the old aunt. His body and face were full of the dark purple poisonous blood. Regardless of the poisonous blood, Yingge quickly wrapped the old aunt's wound so that the poison wouldn't be spread. After it's simply done, the assistant driver yelled, "Damn it! The wild boars came. Get on the train!" Yingge and the stoker carried the old aunt onto the train and closed the door. There's no time to send her to the rear compartment so she had to stay in the engine compartment. As the train was to start, a big wild male boar with a weight of over eight hundred jin jumped onto the tender. Its head was going to reach into the stoker room and it's opening its big mouth to bite the old aunt. At the dangerous moment, smart Yingge took out the red burned iron bar of the stoker from the furnace and stuck it into the wild male boar's mouth. The big wild boar was so painful that it screamed and rolled off the train. The leading boar ran away so it's the same with the remaining wild boars. At this time, the train started up soon. Yingge lifted the brake handle and opened the valve. As the train sped fast, Yingge looked back towards the rear compartments. Oh, damn it! Several big wild boars were trying to break the doors of the passenger compartments to bite and eat people. It's a sheer chaos in the compartments. Women and children cried and shouted. The leaders and working staff were in panic as well. They were bare-handed and had no way of resisting those boars. It's turmoil in the entire compartment.

At this time, Yingge became more proficient and brave. Out of nowhere, he rapidly closed the valve with great force and slammed the brakes on immediately. The wild boars beside the door of the passenger compartments were shaken off the train under strong physical force. Some were crashed to death while some rolled off the slope. In an instant, Yingge opened the valve and lifted the brake handle so that the train could run fast. The wild boars couldn't catch up and they were out of the woods. Soon they arrived at the Forestry Bureau Hospital and the train stopped. They helped the old Korean aunt into the hospital. Yingge took a heavy breath. How terrible it was to think of! At that time, if urgent braking and valve closing were not well operated, the train might have turned over. Then several people may be killed by the train and several might be bit to death by wild boars and wolves. He couldn't explain that. He was scared with cold sweats. Later on, the train kept moving and reached the destination with safety-- the lumber storage yard of Dahai Forestry Bureau.

The locomotive deployment plans of stations were disrupted. The entire bureau was anxiously waiting for the train Yingge drove. All trains were late. The head of the locomotive depot Hu Erpao stamped with fury and yelled, "Who let him stop randomly? I heard there's a woman in the train. It's not appropriate, is it? When he gets back, I will punish him hard. He will be relieved of his post for self-examination. A demerit will be recorded; a criticism meeting will be held or he can be fired. Even prison sentence is possible. I have repeatedly told him that the train is extremely important. No mistake can be made and no delay is allowed. However, he just did the opposite. He's so arrogant. He's the king. How great he is! Nobody dare blame him. He is the one to make decisions. I have to punish him. Bastard, bastard! How terrible it is! There are so many leaders in the train! What if any accident happens? Below Wild Boar Ridge is Sea Wave River where wild boars, wild wolves, tigers and leopards gather here to drink water. Who dare stop there?"

Seeing Yingge, Hu Erpao felt that he couldn't vent his hatred even if he ate him. He questioned directly, "How come you come back? Wild boars are so polite with you. Seems that you have a good relation with them. They actually didn't eat you!" With eyebrows frown and eyes stared, he said ironically, "Who allows you to stop the train halfway and have trains delayed? Do you still bear the rules of locomotive depot on mind? Don't you know how many dangers and worries you have brought to the entire bureau, the deployment office and the locomotive depot?! On the way, wild boars climb onto the compartment. Can you afford the consequences if some of our leaders are bit to death? Will you still be here? Your life is not valuable but it's not the same with provincial and bureau leaders. If anything happens, will I still be here? I may even be sent to prison! Do you know? Oh, my God! You are so audacious that you stop the train at Wild Boar Ridge. You go back for introspection, write a review, confess your mistakes and wait for being punished at the meeting. You want to go to prison, don't you? From now on, you are not allowed to drive the train...... Get out! Who dare hire people like you! I heard there's a woman in the driver's compartment. You dare do that. Seriously?"

Yingge was bombarded with Hu Erpao's criticism before he had time to completely let his nervous nerves relax. He felt wronged and indignant. However, upon closer thinking, he comforted himself that Hu Erpao didn't know the situation so his made sense. He contained his anger, "Sir, you are wrong. It's not a woman. She's an old Korean aunt and was bit by a serpent. She couldn't walk so I stopped the train to save her. However, the wild boars came and there's no time to send her to the passenger compartment. I have to let her stay in the driver's compartment."

Hu Erpao blamed, "Which one is more important? The life of the old aunt or that of the provincial and bureau leaders?" Yingge answered with righteousness, "The old Korean aunt and leaders all belong to our family. All of them matter and should be saved!"

"Damn it! All of them are important!" Hu Erpao repeated and stared Yingge. He sat straight and smoked. "All of them matter? Well, whatever you say!...... Wait to be punished!"

"I just don't understand why he's not afraid of death? Is his life so cheap? I can't believe there are such people in the world. I never heard of it...... It's weird, isnt' it? Anyway, I have to fire him! Otherwise, I don't know how to let the hatred out of my system."

Anyway, the result for Yingge was that he violated the parking rules of the railway department and disrupted the operation schedule. It's good that no casualties were caused. He's going to be severely punished. He would be relieved of his post and sent to the railway legal court for sentencing. How severe it was! His friends were worried about him. The consequences were horrible! In that evening, Yingge was locked in the guard house and relieved of his post for self-examination, waiting to be punished. Several days later, the locomotive depot held a meeting to discuss how to deal with Yingge's violation of the rules. People present at the meeting had their own opinions aired. The deputy head of the locomotive depot rose, "Yingge severely violated the parking rules and disrupted the operation schedule. We suffered great losses. It's quite dangerous. If any casualty was caused, it would have been hard for our head to stay alive. In my opinion, he should be demoted at least and not allowed to drive the train. He should be sent to the forest area to carry logs and reform through labor. I heard that he's a person who fears no death and is not afraid of going to the crematory."

At the critical juncture, the old Korean aunt who was saved came with her son and daughter to the locomotive depot to beg leniency on his savior Yingge. She took some gifts and a long sword as well. She said, "Driver Yingge is my savior. I was bit by a serpent at that time. I would have died of the poison even if I was not eaten by wild boars. I could stay alive all because of Yingge. You can't punish my savior Yingge!" As she was speaking, her face was crowded with tears. She cried, pulled out the long sword and stabbed it onto the table, "I will kill myself here if you punish my savior!"

The sincerity of the old Korean aunt shocked all people present. In the end, Secretary Sun of the forestry bureau stood out and said, "Look. A good turn deserves another. Yingge saved the old Korean aunt and now she's trying to protect her savior. How lofty the friendship is! It's an international spirit. As far as I am concerned, Yingge can't be dismissed. Instead, he should be awarded. He made the right judgment at the life-death moment and chose to stop the train without hesitation. He not only saved the old Korean aunt but also cleverly got rid of the wild boars. The life safety of all people in the compartments was ensured. He successfully drove the train to the destination in the end. How brave he is! At critical moment, he didn't think about his personal interest. What he considered was the safety of others and the entire train! He should be awarded, shouldn't he?" People answered in chorus, "Yes. He can't be fired, let alone reform through labor."

The speech of Secretary Sun made the old Korean aunt lose her sadness and become happy. She was so excited that she led her family to dance joyful Korean dances. Motivated by them, people present danced with them while counting the beats.

5. Mourn for Comrades-in-arms and Classmates

In the marvelous year of 1952 when the war to resist U.S. and aid Korea was fought, our compatriots were sacrificing at the frontline. However, quite a few excellent young people were contributing to support the war at the frontline in the virgin forest of Lesser Khingan Mountains at the frontier of our motherland, the depths of the Snowy Forest. It's covered by snow all the year round with extremely bad conditions.

It's especially cold this winter. The bitter wind cut to the bone and is aggressive in Lesser Khingan Mountains area. The temperature was as low as minus 50-odd. The demand of the frontline for wood kept increasing and there's no time to delay the task of transporting wood. It's extremely dangerous along the route from the mountains to the forest farm. The mountain road was bumpy and the rail was tortuous. The train spiraled up along the mountain road and circled down. It's covered by snow all the year round. How dangerous it was to work in highland. There were many difficulties with lots of accidents. It's hard to guarantee driving safety.

The quality of the railway engines imported in the past was not qualified at all so lots of accidents had happened during the operations. It's either parking overhaul or deviation from the rail and overturn. In case of mudslide that was hard to prevent, stones rolled off the high mountains and blocked the way of the train. It's getting worse. If the train turned over, the furnace was sure to explode, thus destroying the train and killing people. Sometimes the train would be crashed by wild boars coming straight and fall off into the Big Sea Wave River. The train and people all died. Lots of memorial meetings had been held.

Therefore, as long as attendants were chosen to go transport wood, it's hard to ensure that they could come back alive. In that winter, five attendants sacrificed. Some were bit to death by wild boars and wild wolves while some were ran over by stones from the mountains and some fell into the gully and died due to deviation from the rail...... Every task was a life-death test. Old mothers held the hands of their sons. Young wives leaned on their husbands. They were reluctant to part and prayed silently for the safe return of their husbands and sons. Mothers were restless every day and repeatedly told their sons to take care and pay attention to their safety all the time.

Before every task was started, those relatives who saw their beloved ones off would weep and looked worried as if they were parting forever.

One day, Yingge saw his comrades get on the train. The train set out slowly and ran towards the deep mountains. Those weeping relatives didn't go home until the train drove afar and couldn't be seen anymore.

Yingge didn't go home and he walked alone to the tomb of sacrificed comrades silently. He had lots of things to say and let his sadness out of the system.

In one year, Yingge lost five comrades-in-arms and classmates whose voices and expressions were often heard and thought of. Long before they were chatting and talking about their ideal and future with Yingge but now they would rest under the black land forever and never rise. They were still young. The youngest one was only 19. They had parents, brothers, wives and children...... Yingge picked some wild flowers on the way and put them in front of their tombs. He sat in front of his classmate Zhang Jincheng's tomb and reminisced: in that year, the rail sunk and the foundation was not tough so the train derailed and fell into the gully. The train exploded and the miserable scene of his death was vivid in his mind. This was my good brother and classmate. The scene of us talking about our ideal and future often emerged in sight but we just parted with regret. Yingge aguishly talked to his friends who were buried in the grave, "Although you left us, you will always be in our mind. You gloriously sacrificed for people's interest and strength of our motherland. We will keep working hard on the road built by you and complete the cause you haven't finished. People can only live once. When you are alive, you didn't dream away and you weren't unaccomplished. You didn't let down people of our motherland and you died for our people. I can't allow any regret in my own life. As long as they are lofty behaviors, I will do it as you did! As long as it's helpful to people's interest, I will fight for it! As long as it's grand ideal, I will make it come true by working hard! As long as it's a peak which contributes to the construction of our motherland, I will climb it! I will lose no time to live, work and fight because maybe one day I will lie here too due to misfortune, diseases, unexpected natural diaster and accidents during driving. By then, I will have no opportunity to fight, work hard and climb. Hence, as long as I am alive for one day and I can still breathe, I will live, work and study with passion just like you did in the past. Let the time and history test me! Farewell, my old friend! My old classmate!"

With tears in his eyes, Yingge stoop up, grabbed a handful of soil from the tomb and clasped it in hand...... It seemed that he was holding the hands of his classmates and comrades-in-arms.

Yingge bowed for three times in front of his late old classmate, reluctant to leave. He bore infinite pains on the inner side. He returned rapidly after walking for a few steps, laid on his old classmate Zhang Jincheng's tomb and cried, "I am leaving. May you rest at peace, my brother! I need to go to work."

With deep memory of his classmates and comrades-in-arms cherished in mind and promise in front of them borne in mind, Yingge wiped off his tears with great pain and left the cemetery.

On the way back to the dorm, Yingge thought a lot, "What's the most precious thing in a lifetime? It's life. People can live once only. As long you die, you will lie there and can never rise and never have the opportunity to serve people and fight for the strength of your motherland."

"In the era full of uncertain dangers, it's hard to forecast your future. Nobody knows when you will come across dangers in the process of transporting wood. Maybe there's misfortune, sudden and unpredictable conditions which may instantly take your life. Then you can never fight and contribute." Thinking of this, Yingge stood up and wiped off his tears. "No! I need to go to work now. I will meet difficult challenges!" He left the cemetery rapidly.

Yingge's companions were waiting for him in the dorm. Little Ma asked, "Where have you been? We have been waiting for you to have meals. How come you come back so late? What happened?...... What? Did your eyes swell?"

Yingge said, "I went to visit an old classmate Zhang Jincheng in the cemetery...... I have missed him so much recently. Every time before the task, I miss him. He keeps popping up in my mind and I can't stay calm. I am restless."

Accidents of turnover remained constant in the locomotive depot. Death was common occurrence. In the rainy season, mudslide stones rolled off the mountains to destroy the train and vehicles. The drivers and attendants came across wild boars when they repaired the train on the way. It's also common for wild wolves to injure people. It's virgin forest so wild beasts were extremely furious. It's a place which had never been treaded in the past decades and past several hundred years. It's sparsely populated. It's not rare and it's normal that accidents of people being bit by wild beasts happen.

It's a dangerous place but Yingge possessed the personalities of Shandong people and persistence in his cause. He always maintained that people could only live once and fight for few times so he wasn't intimidated by these evil situations.

He said to his driver partner, "We are indeed confronted with difficulties ahead. Should we lie idle just because of difficulties? What do the Party and country send us for? Death befalls all men but when your death is as heavy as Mount Tai, your death is worth it. Then go for it and don't be terrified!"

Given constant occurrence of accidents, it's hard to complete the tasks of transporting wood from the mountains, which further affects the entire situation and the fight at the frontline! We need to solve relevant problems in the transportation process. It's the current priority to prevent the occurrence of accidents.

He continued, "When I studied in Northeast Forest Industry Technical College, I was very interested in mechanics and physics, etc. so I had good performance in them. Our attendant team need to actively shoulder the responsibility and face the difficulty. In order to build our motherland, we not only need to work harder but also apply our knowledge to work ingeniously. We need to drive with scientific ideologies and we need to research on site, investigate reasons for occurrence of accidents, look for solutions and lay a good foundation for the later generation so as to achieve the goals of fast transportation, few accidents and zero death."

Little Ma said, "In my opinion, there are indeed several sections with dangerous topography and great difficulty along the rail route. Moreover, it's winter when the road was paved that year. Schedule was tight and lots of hidden accident dangers were left."

Yingge said, "Among them, the most important sections are Wild Boar Ridge, Frog Pond, Wild Wolf Den and Huolonggou Gully where it's most likely to cause accidents with their large slope, numerous turns and soft road foundations. The train vibrates when they are running so stones drop from the mountains. The rail is either broken or buried."

One day, Yingge went report to Secretary Li with his sincerity and responsibility for the cause, "Now the locomotive depot indeed faces difficulties. Drivers think the difficulties are great. It's hard to assign the driving task. People say they have urgent things to do so they can't accept the tasks. It's difficult and dangerous, which is true because continuous accidents make drivers horrified. The head of the locomotive depot is quite frustrated and often loses his temper. He abuses anyone! He said, 'I can't take care of this anymore. Whoever is willing to take my post, take it. I will leave my hand.'"

Secretary Li said, "Comrade Yingge, you are right. There are too many difficulties so far for the locomotive depot. Lots of accidents and casualties are witnessed. It's really difficult! I have no idea!"

Yingge said, "Yes. The difficulties objectively exist in our locomotive depot at present. People are afraid of accepting the task and they are in panic! Secretary Li, it's difficult to get anyone for the task. All of them fear death. Indeed it's dangerous. Although we should face difficulties, we should act it out. There's no condition for performing the task so we need to create conditions. Otherwise, how can we overcome difficulties? How can we complete the task of wood transportation? What do we use to support the war to resist U.S. and aid Korea?"

Yingge continued, "Secretary Li, please give us your instruction! Please send my attendant team to investigate in the mountains first and look for the reasons for the occurrence of accidents."

"Just as what I said earlier, surveys should be made first with a scientific attitude. A League member should not talk about good things only. Let's see actions in face of difficulty! The reasons should be found out so as to pave a way for smooth fulfillment of transportation tasks." Young Yingge was so excited that he emphasized before the Secretary, "It's time for us League members to contribute."

Secretary Li held Yingge's hands tightly and he was so moved that his eyes were filled with tears, "Yingge! Good comrade! Good boy! Boy, go investigate with your scientific attitude and locate the reasons for accidents. The Party believes in you and knows that you will complete the task. But I am also worried! It's dangerous to stop the train for investigation at some sections where accidents often happen. You must be careful...... You have your parents and siblings." Tears coursed down the cheeks of Secretary Li as he was speaking, "Go! I am really worried. Be careful. Wish you a success!"

Every time when this was talked, Yingge was especially carried away. At that time, the rapidly running train needed to go through cliffs and steep mountains. Frog Pond was an incident-packed place and there's a danger of turnover anytime. Once accidents occurred, drivers would lie under the black land forever. They were the spiritual motivation for Yingge to stick to exploration all the time.

6. Tigers Jumping onto the Locomotive

Yingge said goodbye to Secretary Li and next day, his attendant team including two members and he went to see the head Hu Erpao and reported to him the opinions of Secretary Li. Hu Erpao didn't say too much, "You take care of your safety during the accident investigation. Those sections which are to be investigated are not those places where you take your beloved girls to travel. Watch out those wild wolves and tigers. They might attack you."

The sections which Yingge and his two partners were to investigate were indeed dangerous and many accidents had happened in those places in the past.

They planned to visit other sections where accidents often occurred on the way and check whether there were hidden dangers or not.

The key work in the end was to check Frog Pond where they stopped the train. They walked along the rail and examined it. They found that some parts of the rail sunk and the surfaces between two rails were uneven, which was the origin of accident occurrence. It's pond here so the road foundation was soft. There's no problem in winter when the soil was frozen. However, in other seasons of the year, especially in rainy days, it's easy for the rail to sink when the train which carried wood passed here. If overhaul was not often made, turnover accidents would be likely to happen. Hence, the track maintenance division needed to send people to check the rails on a regular basis. There's water, weeds and little fish in the pond. In particular, in spring, quite a few ducks came to lay eggs and incubated little ducks. It's also the place where wild animals drank water and some of them looked for duck eggs in the weeds. Therefore, it's the place where wild boars, tigers and wild wolves had fun. We were checking and repairing the sleeper on the sinking foundation. As we were going to finish the work, the assistant driver Little Liu suddenly found that a big tiger which was over two meters was running towards us from the front left of the train. Little Liu shouted, "Damn it! Here comes a tiger! Get on the train quickly!" Under Yingge's cover, they went into the train and Yingge got on in the end. While closing the iron door, his coat was clamped in the door. The tiger bit his coat and Yingge immediately opened the valve. The train started and white steam spurted from the cylinder drainer. The heat forced the tiger to drop Yingge's coat. The tiger laid there and couldn't see the train's direction. At this time, Yingge opened the valves more and the train ran rapidly. Later, the tiger was clear about where the train was running and caught up with the train. The tiger jumped onto the locomotive engine which was so hot that forced the tiger jump to the tender from the driver's compartment roof. Then it stayed

there still as if it's a customer. Everything was fine and the train was running fast. The tiger turned back and his ass aimed at the driver's compartment. The three of them were terrified. If the tiger stayed there and didn't go away, what should they do when they arrived the train station? Many people were waiting for the train at the station. It would be too dangerous if the tiger jumped off the train. It might bit several people to death. What if it took away a child? It would be severe. Anyway they had to drive the tiger off the train. The assistant driver Little Liu said, "Yingge Dache, stop the train and I will drive the tiger off." Yingge said, "No way! Can you fight the tiger? Are you better than the Tiger Killer at Jingyanggang? Come one, don't go for death!"

Yingge showed resourcefulness in an emergency. He inserted the two-meter-odd iron bar which was used for the furnace into the furnace to burn it red. Yingge broke the glass window of the tender, took out the red iron bar and passed it through the window of the tender. While driving the train fast, Yingge turned around to forcefully penetrate the red iron bar into the asshole of the tiger which screamed and jumped off the train. The tiger ran, roared and ran into the dense forest. It was followed by two small tigers. Over 20 minutes later, the train arrived at the train station ahead. Lots of people at the platform came up, "What a hero to drive off the tiger!" Hearing the incident, the director general and Secretary Li came to hug Yingge, shook hands with him and shouted, "You did a good job! You are our hero!" The accident was caused by untimely overhaul by the track maintenance division, and the reasons for accidents in Frog Pond were located as well. The director general said to Mr. Ma, head of the track maintenance division, "Here's the order for track maintenance division. Tomorrow send an engineer team to check and repair the sections where accidents happened. Frog Pond is a dangerous area where there are many wild animals. Take two machines guns so that you can protect yourselves if you come across lots of wild animals on the way. Am I understood? Do what I said!" Mr. Ma answered, "Yes, sir! We will do as you said!"

Secretary Li said, "If Yingge didn't drive the tiger away on the way, people's lives would have been endangered at the station. It would be too dangerous."

Hu Erpao put on a grand air, "Look, every time when an accident happened, the locomotive depot was blamed. This time your track maintenance department should shoulder the responsibility. Ah! Our good Yingge. You are our hero! You found out the reasons for accidents. Good! Cool!" People dispersed happily. Since then, Yingge had left the "footprint" of fighting against tigers on the train.

6. New Technology Earned by Life

Two months later, director general Yuan of the forestry bureau came to the locomotive depot. He served as the deputy commander in the war to resist U.S. and aid Korea. His words and deeds were of emotional appeal. He carried out his task with drive and sweep. Besides, he was good at motivating people. He presided over a full-section safety production and transportation meeting. People who attended the meeting included division heads, heads of stations, general chief dispatcher, major leaders of electricity division, track maintenance division and vehicle division as well as drivers and attendants of the entire locomotive depot.

Director general Yuan said, "At present the production task of our bureau is not fulfilled yet. Provincial, municipal and forestry bureau leaders pay special attention to it. They are anxious! The fight at the frontline is quite intense. They need our forestry bureau to produce enough wood for building bridges and trenches, and repairing roads. However, the driving safety can't be ensured so it's difficult to transport wood. Hence, today we hold this meeting to discuss how we can solve the current problem of driving safety, locate causes for accidents and parking in the hope of coming up with a good safe driving and transportation plan."

"Recently comrade Yingge has risked his life to perform driving tasks for several times. Through several actual surveys, he found out the reasons for accident occurrence during the trial transportation and concluded a feasible transportation plan. You are invited here to discuss it today. Hopefully you can talk whatever you want and let's hear your opinions. Anyway our goal is safe driving in future."

The first driver who stood up was Rash Fellow Yang who was a young man. Once he jumped from the train in face danger and had a narrow escape. He had been healing at home in the past few months. His legs broke so he attended the meeting on a crutch.

"I heard at home that Yingge Dache (driver) proposed some new theories and new driving methods. Personally I don't think these theories in book such as mechanics laws, Newton theory and inertia law, etc., whatever, work for us. They are theories innovated by foreigners. Did foreigners drive our train? Did they come to site? In my opinion, the new driving methods are a bit risky. Rapid operation down the hill is thrilling. The train almost flies."

Dache Wang followed, "According to Yingge's driving theory, we shouldn't close the valve and lower the brake; instead, we are required to fully opcn the valve and lift the brake to let the train speed up. The train is flying, which is terrible. It won't be easy to ensure safety by then. If the train derails, it will bump against mountains or fall into the Big Sea Wave River. We need to cherish our lives. I think the plan needs to be further studied. We have witnessed lots of accidents in which both people and the train were destroyed."

Next, Driver Guan stood up, "Few months ago when Dache Tang performed the driving task, the training was running down a great slope with over 40 compartments at Frog Pond section. However, wild boars showed up. In order not to let them catch up, he drove so fast, forgot to close the valve and lower the brake. The running train sped along so rapidly that it's going to turn over and fall into the Big Sea Wave River. Seeing the urgent situation, the assistant driver and stoker jumped into the Big Sea Wave River. They were badly injured with broken legs and twisted waists. They were still in the hospital now. Dache Tang was so scared that he sat down straight beside the brake machine and waited for death. He even peed and pooed in his pants, and became mentally disordered. He even didn't know the train arrived at the station, and just said, 'Watch out! Watch out!' He ended up running three red lights. Fortunately, the train didn't hit the trains at the station. The situation was really horrible and scaring. If the deployment division didn't order stations needed to avoid the 311 train and asked the heads to pay attention, dozens of people in the trains would have been killed in the crash. Explosion would have been caused to destroy the trains and kill people. Now Dache Tang is still in the madhouse and every day he shouts, 'Watch out! Watch out......' He kept his eyes wide open but didn't say anything and couldn't take care of himself. Isn't it a lesson to learn? We should think about it! You know, director general. Dache Tang could stop the train because there's no steam in the furnace. The pressure is less and the wheels stopped. That's it."

The director general said, "We need to take into account detailed situations, analyze them based on concrete conditions and look for causes. We can think about that. The track maintenance division should pay attention to overhaul at the Frog Pond section."

Hu Erpao, deputy head of the locomotive depot squinted his eyes and said in a weird way, "I am not opposed to new theories, new methods and laws for transportation. In the past, the task of 35 to 40 compartments of wood for each train even couldn't be fulfilled. Now it's reduced to 15 to 20 compartments for each train with rapid speed. How come the task can be completed? Besides, the less the transported wood, the fewer the drivers' bonus. There won't be commissions for employees of the entire locomotive depot. We have to think about their benefits! We can't just brag, which is worthless."

Deputy director general Chi rose, "At this meeting, both positive and negative opinions can be proposed. We should put our heads together. While talking about Yingge's new ideas and opinions, we should discuss other new methods and introduce new experience so as to ensure safe transportation and fulfillment of wood transportation tasks. We are at a dead end. If we can't complete our tasks, how can we explain to the soldiers who are safeguarding our country and face death unflinchingly at the frontline? If so, it means we leaders are incompetent and useless. Does anyone have something to say? If no, Yingge can tell us your opinion."

Yingge stood up and looked around. People quited down and stopped whispering.

Yingge put on a confident air, "Leaders and comrades, I would like to report to you. In the past few months, I have performed the driving task to transport wood in person. My surveys which included many aspects concluded causes for accident occurrence in the past and put forward some new methods and opinions."

Yingge emphasized, "It's naturally important to complete the transportation task but the task schedule should be made based on actual conditions and the capacity of our bureau. If the tasks are set without thinking about safety and the actual conditions of the locomotive depot, it could only burden people. Fulfillment of tasks is out of the question without safety. There are certain problems in the tasks of our locomotive depot. The track maintenance division and vehicle division don't go to the site and fail to consider the current conditions and capabilities of our locomotive depot. Problems exist in other divisions either except locomotive depot. Different divisions have done a bad job in ensuring safe driving. We just ignored workers' lives in order to perform tasks. We give them too much pressure. That's why accidents happened one after another. Drivers dare not accept the driving tasks. How terrible it is! Mr. Liu is a good worker! Zhang Bin is an able young man. In order to transport more wood and run rapidly, the train derailed and exploded. They fell off the cliff and died in the gully, leaving the old mother with diseases and two children at home. The mother cried for his son. How miserable it is! Many families suffered from such misery. It's because the track maintenance division failed to check and repair the rails. We should adjust the transportation tasks. At present, there are many problems with the trains of the locomotive depot and many spare parts of the trains in the vehicle division were damaged and lack of repair. So the vehicle division should also conduct overhaul on a regular basis. The track maintenance division had more problems. The rails are uneven so the train can't run steadily. The spaces between rails are different and the space is too great at the joints. Quite a few dog-head spikes were pulled out at the sleepers of the rails. It's likely to cause turnover. The track maintenance division should check and repair sections where accidents occurred along the way. Many damaged trains can't be used and lie idle in the garage. They will be driven in case of emergency in order to complete tasks. Leaders of different divisions, we can't just think about tasks only, can we? How about now? Did we complete our tasks?" As Yingge spoke, he got carried away.

The director general chipped in, "Good. You did an appropriate survey, found out many factors influencing safety. Your opinions are valuable and appreciated!"

Yingge went straight to the heart of the problem, "Our locomotive depot and leaders can't just focus on bonus, output value and profits, and moreover can't ignore the lives of workers at the front line for the sake of pure commissions. Our trains are getting old and lack of overhaul. Many spare parts need to changed. That's why accidents often occur on the way of transportation, our train stops halfway for repair and staff often come across wild beasts from the mountains which bit people at night. Dache Ma was so strong but he was bit to death by wild boars while repairing the train at night. Have we made introspection over this?"

The director general interposed, "Well said! It's right!"

Yingge continued, "I am enlightened by their rapid train operation but without key turnover accidents. I have fully and carefully studied the entire process of driving, and concluded one method, that is, when the train is running down a slope, we need to open the valve and lift the brake. It's also concluded from the lesson learned from several accidents such as falling off the cliff, and falling into the river and exploding which caused casualties. In particular, on the way of driving, I stopped to check the road conditions and further find out multiple causes for turnover accidents. Once, I stopped the train at Wild Boar Ridge to check whether the rails were parallel or not and whether stones would roll off the mountains to destroy the rails or not. It's really dangerous to stop the train there. Wild boars ran towards us. It's good that little Feng, the driver, found it in time and got me on the train immediately, thus avoiding the consequence of being bit to death by wild boars."

"I learn this from my own experience. Later, I drove the train for 12 times and still kept fast speed. As long as mountain stones were not in thc way on the rail and there's no problem with the rails, it's fine to pull 20 to 25 compartments and we could drive the train every three days. It takes a long time to load the train if 40 compartments are pulled. It takes one week to drive once but now I can drove twice in one week and transport the same amount of wood. Moreover, safety is the most important. Fulfillment of tasks is out of the question without safety." The director general chipped in again, "You are right. We need to put safety first! It's precious experience. It's experience earned by life!"

Yingge followed, "I learned it from the book. According to Newton's laws of motion in physics, external force brings about accelerated speed. The dynamics remain constantly dynamic and the statics remain constantly static. Let's go back to the features of our trains and their structure features. When the brake is lowered, the train will slow down right away and stop. However, there's no brake in the compartments but it still maintains its accelerated speed. Without braking, the farther it runs, the faster it is. With accelerated speed, if the valve is closed in the locomotive engine and the brake is lowered, the locomotive engine will slow down. Then the compartments behind don't slow down and the accelerated speed still exists. The father it runs, the faster it is. Hence, the entire train still running forward with high speed."

Yingge analyzed, "Under strong impact of dozens of compartments, the locomotive engine probably derails and charges towards the cliff. The hooks which connect the compartments will be pressed tight one after another. They will get tighter. Soon, the wood in the compartments will be squeezed to the locomotive engine, thus leading to the train's deviation from the rails and into the Big Sea Wave River as well as destroyed train and dead people. Think about it. Am I right? Isn't it the actual condition?" Yingge supplemented.

People whispered to each other and discussed. Some of them shook their heads while some showed approval with their eyes and some were not convinced yet. Yingge continued, "We can look at it from another perspective. When the train is running downhill, if we don't close the valve and lower the brake, and we let the train run forward along the rail, then the hooks which connect compartments are tightened one by one. Compartments charge forward at an accelerated speed. The speed of the compartments is the same with that of the locomotive engine. In this way, compartments won't thrust towards the engine and the front compartment won't bump against the locomotive engine either. The locomotive engine runs normally without derailing. If fewer compartments are pulled, the squeeze strength between compartments will be weaker, the impulsion will be gone and the possibility of turnover is smaller."

The director general held Yingge's hands and said with emotions, "Comrades, Yingge has risked his life and contributed to create a new way with revolutionary spirits. He made experiments, conducted surveys and concluded a successful way of driving that is suitable for local conditions with scientific methods. Besides, he located the causes for dangers. After hearing what he said, I found it made much sense. I was so moved. In future, vehicle division, track maintenance division and locomotive depot, etc. should work harder on overhaul, go to the sites and conduct studies with scientific ideologies so as to solve existing problems in the section. Leaders at different levels should go to the production site and the basic level to discover problems, solve difficulties, value safety and fulfill production tasks. The leaders at the lower level should be responsible for failure to complete tasks but the superior leaders should bear greater responsibilities!"

"All of us should keep Yingge's motto in mind: we shouldn't fear difficulties if we want revolution. It's because of difficulties that we need you to solve them. Ideologies are not enough for innovation and scientific researches. At critical moments, we should have the spirit of dedication. Yingge has risked his life to stop the train along the way and conduct surveys in different dangerous sections, thus locating causes for unsafety."

7. Love Storm

Ministry of Agriculture and Forestry gave Dahai Forestry Bureau a quota of five people who could go to college. One of them was assigned by the forestry bureau to Yingge whose inner side was full of conflicts and argument after he learned about it. He had been adapted to the life in the forest area and had a desirable girlfriend. He thought it's sweet and happy. He wanted to work in the forest area in the rest of his life and give up the opportunity for going to college. Otherwise, he would feel guilty about his girlfriend's true love and care. Just as the famous saying went, "life is dear, love is dearer."

One day afternoon, the couple was walking on a shady path. Yingge told his internal conflicts to Feng Qinqin. Qinqin was shocked and thought Yingge actually wanted to abandon the opportunity for going to college and his personal prospect for the sake of love. On the one hand, she admired Yingge's loyalty to love, pure moral quality, persistence and exploration of his cause, but on the other hand, she's worried about Yingge's future.

Feng Qinqin had an agile thought. In order to motivate Yingge, she became angry instead of being happy, started at him and criticized, "You are such a short-sighted man. You don't have your ideal and aren't worth my love!" She turned around without looking back. She wept and ran away......

Little Yingge stood there and was at a loss after being blamed. It's been a long while before he could wake up. He asked himself whether it's right or not to abandon his prospect and give up his ideal and the opportunity for college for the sake of his girlfriend! He said to himself, "She's right! She should be angry with me!"

Yingge was of impatient disposition. Once he's bent on doing something, he would take actions. He decided to lose no time to review what he's learned. He cherished the opportunity for college so much. He spent his spare time and break time during work in studying.

In the afternoon of next day, Liu Lihua, daughter of director general Liu of the forestry bureau where Yingge worked for came to Yingge's dorm. Yingge was busy preparing his studies. She's the head nurse of the hospital and her love for Yingge could be described by obsession. She often went to the locomotive depot to chat with Yingge. Young workers laughed at her, "You can't live without Yingge!" A young man said, "I love her but she didn't love me. What should I do?" The young man sent out a burst of laughters. She tried to persuade Yingge to keep working in the forest area and drove off those young men who pursued her. She ignored them and loved none of them. Her entire heart focused on Yingge.

Yingge was devoted to his study and didnt' notice Little Liu entered the room. She stood behind Yingge and said, "Look at you. You even don't want to talk to me since you are going to college. 'You are immortal', huh? Look at the airs you put on. You are not a college student yet."

Yingge stood up immediately, "I'm really sorry. I didn't see you. I am doing a maths problem. Please forgive me! Something wrong?"

Little Liu said, "Nothing special. I just come to see you. Am I not welcomed?"

"Thank you! Welcome!" Yingge said.

Little Liu said, "My father said you are talented and educated. If you can work in the forest area, you will be the next head of the locomotive depot, which is more promising than going to college. I will definitely help you. Maybe in future you can become the deputy director general and even the director general! It's all up to you."

Yingge refused, "Little Liu! You are wrong. I am not suitable for being a leader. I can only serve others like driving which is my profession. I am not qualified for being a leader and directing others. I never think of that!"

"Don't be modest. My father says you can and you can. You have my father help you. What are you afraid of? You will do better than them."

"I still want to go to college. I will have a try this year. If I fail this time, I will take the exam next year. I don't believe I can't pass it. Where there's a will, there's a way. As long as I make up my mind, perseverance will prevail."

Little Liu was getting angrier and thought Yingge was unappreciative. He would rather become a poor student than being promoted to serve as an officer. He's "corny" and an "ox which ate grass". Little Liu thought her "good intention" was failed. As the daughter of the director general, her spoiled bad temper broke out. "Clang". She slapped Yingge, "Go to your college! I have backed the wrong horse in the past two years. Damn your poverty! Bye, college student. You will regret! Old ox! Corny man!"

Yingge thought to himself: It's really hard to fathom what girls think. He was blamed by Feng for not wanting to go to college but was slapped by Liu for going to college. Yingge knew well that no mater who beat or blame her, it's out of "love" and "too much love leads to hatred". Beat me! It's a kind of liberation. I was sure to go to college. However, he's still perplexed. He strolled alone in the forest while humming a sad song. In the serene mountain forest, he meditated, lingered, was frustrated and confused...... He sung lightly and slow and romantic sound resonated in the forest.

Liu cried and ran to her father, the director general. She felt wronged, "Yingge said he must go to college and leave the forest area. Why don't you promote him to the leader earlier? Maybe he would have loved me. It's all your fault!" She still abused Yingge and hated him, saying he's a "bumpkin".

Director general Liu regarded his daughter as the apple of his eye. He heard his daughter out with patience and said amiably to her, "My baby love, don't worry. He won't pass the exam. It's not that easy. Last year, I chose ten young men to take the exam and none of them passed it. This year, I only approved five. Think about it. Is it possible? It's too hard for a working man to pass the exam. Don't cry. Let him take the exam. We'll see."

"Dad! I slapped Yingge to let my anger out of the system". Liu said. Her father said, "Oh, this is your fault. A watched pot never boils. Go apologize to him when you are free. Love is not out of beating. When I was young and pursued some girl, I would knee down...... Look at you. You even beat him. It's not reasonable, isn't it? Say sorry to Yingge when you have time."

8. Fly the Dream

Since last time when Feng Qinqin denounced Yingge, she had been like a student who did something wrong and waited for the teacher to call her for criticism. She's extremely sad and restless all the day, not knowing how to apologize to Yingge and ask for his forgiveness. One day, little Feng came to see Yingge with a piece of newspaper which was about college exam. Little Feng worked at the statistics office of the bureau so she read newspapers every day. She's well informed and knew a lot. Little Feng said to Yingge, "Do you still bear grudges against my denouncement? Please forgive me. I was trying to encourage you, which was overdone. However, I bring some good news today to make it up. This year, you can sign up for the college entrance exam. The conditions are loose this year. Sign-up priority is given to people with technical titles. If you pass the exam, you can study in college while being paid. It's a rare opportunity. Anyway, you can't miss it. There's another good thing for you: those who are labor models, advanced workers, innovators and contributors at work can sign up first. You are an advanced employee of our bureau with innovations. You work hard in daily time. I am confident you can pass it. You must sign up for it."

Yingge said, "Will the superior leader allow me to sign up for it?"

Feng Qinqin said to Yingge, full of tenderness, “You can talk with him. You have always wanted to go to college for further study, then go abroad and achieve a doctoral degree, haven’t you? Where’s your determination now? You must take the exam. It doesn’t matter if you fail. Just have a try.”

Yingge went to discuss it with Liu Cheng and asked him whom they should go for approval if he wanted to sign up. They seriously analyzed the situation: It’s off season for production at present. It’s the time when the track maintenance division repaired road foundations so there were few driving tasks. We could say to our leader, “We just go have a try. We know we won’t pass the exam and just want to check our current leve. We will be back after one week.”

First they needed to meet the depot head Hu Erpao because he’s in charge of production and they had to obtain his approval.

Seeing Yingge and Liu Cheng coming, Hu Erpao asked with eyeballs aside, “What are you here for? One never goes to the temple for nothing. Just tell me straight. People don’t take off their pants for breaking wind. You intellectuals always beat around the bush. Even if you are off the topic, you can still get back to it. Am I right? It doesn’t matter whether you speak good or bad.” Hu Erpao was like this: He’s honest and kind-hearted. Anyway, no matter what he said, it was always harsh to the listeners.

Yingge said solemnly, “We have something that needs your approval. We want to sign up for college entrance exam. We just want to have a try and see whether you have any instruction or not.”

Hu Erpao said, “I have nothing to say except: first, you guys can’t go. The team needs you. Who will shoulder the responsibility if you leave? Especially Yingge can’t leave. Second, instruction? There’s nothing to tell. What you need to do is work hard here and complete your tasks and production. This is the only thing I know. Here’s all what I want to say. Am I understood? Attention! Turn backward! March!”

Yingge's idea was put a damper on by Hu Erpao and he returned, crestfallen. However, he was not reconciled to it. Soon, he went to Secretary Li to hear his opinions.

Yingge came to the office of Secretary Li and talked about his ideas and requirements. Different from Hu Erpao, Secretary Li was always so amiable ad easy-going.

Secretary Li answered, "Comrade Yingge, it's good thing to sign for the college entrance exam and have further studies. Our country falls short of advanced personnel. You need to acquire greater knowledge if you want to make achievements in technologies, innovate and create new things. However, graduating from the technical college, you are almost the most learned man in our locomotive depot. You have contributed a lot to the development of the locomotive depot and solved lots of difficult problems in the transportation. What a great performance! Our locomotive depot needs you very much and can't leave you. If you really want to have a try, I am not opposed to it. You can go but you need to arrange the tasks and work orderly."

In the eyes of Secretary Li, it's no easy job to pass the college entrance exam for people on the job who were usually busy and didn't have time to review. It's really difficult. Now one out of dozens of people and even a hundred people could succeed. "I don't think you can pass but anyway, have a try!" Secretary Li agreed because he didn't want to discourage them and they would give up when they failed and came back. He's truly the secretary and leader. He had a strategy in terms of speaking and acting. Secretary Li's name was Li Ming and was sent here to take charge of the secretary work in the League after graduation. He's upright and honest in daily behaviors. Besides, he dared to speak and act with tough spirits.

Yingge and Liu Cheng performed several driving tasks with success.

After preparation, they left the locomotive depot for the town to sign up for the college entrance exam.

They inquired at the sign-up office, only three days left. They were a bit late because they needed to go through a lot of procedures: letter of introduction from the institution, letter of introduction from the general bureau, appraisal of work performance in the institution and personnel archives of the original institution, which almost took over a week.

It seemed that they couldn't sign up and had missed the opportunity this year.

Yingge thought to himself on the way back home: It's fine. Where there's a life, there's a hope. They can sign up next year. He and Liu Cheng heard from their friend that a cram class just began. After discussion, they decided to learn something which they failed to acquire before since they were here. They would wait for the opportunity next year.

As long as one had knowledge and determination, you didn't need to fear there's no opportunity. Even if you didn't go to college, it would be helpful to future work and technological reform with these new knowledge and information. They can be applied anyway so it's with the railway.

They made up their mind. It's early winter. Northeast China had a longer winter and it snowed already in October. They rented a roof shed where sundries and wood were stored. There's only a small door. The wind came from all directions. Today's water froze next day.

They lived here for three weeks in total which already surpassed the leave they asked for. They hadn't finished the study. It's too cold but they didn't have money to buy heavy clothes. They paid the tuition with their money. They lived on bread. Therefore, they couldn't stay here anymore and had to return to the locomotive depot of the forest area.

Seeing them back, Hu Erpao teased, "Hahah, you are finally back. Little birds went out for food but failed and returned hungry. I thought you went to college to work as principal and experts with your doctoral degree. Why are you back? You don't have anything to eat? We can't hire such big potatoes like you. You are back late. According to the rules of the locomotive depot, you are fired. Turn backward and march!"

Yingge felt ashamed to see Secretary Li. The two of them went back to their dorm. Comrades cared them a lot. Some asked them questions and some offered methods to encourage them.

It's almost eight. Yingge and Liu Cheng walked on the snow field, climbed little hills and came to the dorm of the general bureau. They knocked the door and the wife of the director general opened the door for them.

They kneed down after entering the house and said to director general Yuan, "We are here to confess and ask for punishment." Director general Yuan was confused and didn't know what happened to Yingge. He asked him immediately, "Little Yingge, you are the advanced worker. What happened? What crime did you commit? Murder...... Set fire...... Tell me, what did you do?"

"We are back late because we went to sign up for the college entrance exam. We are fired." Director general Yuan came to realize the truth, "I though you committed crime. It's about college entrance exam which is nothing bad. It's a good thing. Other people dare not go even. If one doesn't have certain knowledge, he is afraid. Get on your feet. You are talents of our country. You are not sinful at all. People should learn from you. Yingge is a good comrade and the great hero of our bureau. Hahah, confess? There's nothing to confess...... Hahahah....." Director general Yuan laughed back and forth, "If I let them go take the exam, will they have the courage?" The director general said, "It's funny! Who fired you?" Yingge said, "The head Mr. Hu doesn't want us to work." The director general said, "They are crazy. They are mad. I am calling him right now. You go back and prepare to go to work tomorrow. Go talk with Secretary Li. If they ask, you just tell them it's my order."

"Is this Old Hu? Are you crazy! Why don't let Yingge go to work? Who asks you to fire him? Don't you listen to me? Did you ask me? You made the decision? Domineering! Liberalism!"

"Let comrade Yingge to go work tomorrow. If there's a driving task, give it to him. Such good comrade can't be fired randomly. What will we do with our country's construction but for talents? Next time if you have such liberalism behaviors, I will dismiss you. Do you understand? Do what I said!"

Next day, Yingge came to see the head Hu Erpao in the locomotive depot. "Oh, my God. You are awesome! I dare not offend you. I failed to recognize a great person. You repot to the director general who almost fired me. I was so angry that day. I was just kidding. Will I fire you without the approval of superior leaders? Don't be mad. Work hard. You can go take a rest for two days. It's not busy in the locomotive depot recently. The trains are being checked and repaired. Don't take it seriously. Just do me a favor, will you?" Hu Erpao saw them to the door while patting their backs. Yingge and Liu Cheng went back to their dorm. Comrades asked, "What did Hu Erpao say to you?"

Liu Cheng repeated what Hu Erpao said to them which triggered a burst of laughters, "Hu Erpao has always feared the strong and bullied the weak. Anyone who was caught by him would have suffered. Yingge is not only our hero of driving but also a hero who fights against Old Hu." After that, they again roared with laughters.

9. Learn for People and Learn for the Construction of Motherland

Yingge walked out of the dining hall with a double-layer lunchbox in his hand: one layer was for greens and one for rice. Today he didn't have any task. He had on shift for two days and two nights. This time he had a long off-work time so he could concentrate on his study and review the physics homework he didn't finish two days ago. Yingge and Liu Cheng came to the jungle and folded two pieces of newspapers on the green grassland. They sat down. It's quiet here. They were doing homework while reading the book. Time for learning was squeezed out just like the water in the sponge which could still be obtained as long as you squeezed it. So it's the same with learning time. They had to lose no time to study because time flied unconsciously day by day, month by month and year by year......

Yingge said, "Liu Cheng, we are still young. The science knowledge we grasp is far from sufficient for our work. We need to reform technologies and make some achievements if we want to do a good job. We have to study. Now there are many accidents and problems in the transportation because we fall short of science knowledge. In future, if there's an opportunity, I still want to go to college for further study. Our knowledge is not equal to requirements. We know few theories, which limit the improvement of our business level and our work!" After reading for several hours, they talked about some physics problems. Unconsciously, the sun set. Liu Cheng said, "Let's go back for dinner! There's some hot water in the room." Yingge said, "You go back first! I want to study more here! When it gets dark, I can use my flashlight. It's okay. It's noisy in the room and I couldn't concentrate on my study."

"Tomorrow there's no time to rest. In the morning, the technology seminar will be held and the train needs to be repaired in the afternoon. You go back first!" Yingge sat there and read the book. Many mosquitoes constantly bit Yingge's hands. He beat the mosquitoes with the tree branch in his hand while reading.

Feng Qinqin went to the dorm to see Yingge. Little Ma saw her, "Oh, welcome, beauty. Are you missing Yingge Dache?" Little Ma joked. Little Feng went up to beat him. He ran and said, "If you don't beat me, I will tell you where he is." "Okay! I stop but I will beat you if you get naughty again." "Yingge Dache is waiting for you in the small jungles at the east of Big Sea Wave River." Feng Qinqin blamed, "Bullshit. You want me to beat you, don't you?" "I am telling you the truth. Why are you still beating me. Well, leave it if you don't trust me." Little Feng walked towards the riverside with uncertainty. She looked around and finally found Yingge. She shouted, "Yingge, what are you doing there!"

Hearing Feng Qinqin's voice, Yingge felt it so amiable and sweet, "I am here. Watch out. Don't be tip over the tree branches." Feng Qinqin said, "It's so late. Why are you still here?"

Yingge said to Feng Qinqin in a kind way, "How did you know I am here?"

"I just know it. I can predict. Don't you know it?"

Yingge said, "You are really learned. You are like Zhuge Liang and can foresee the future." Yingge and Feng Qinqin were strolling along the Sea Wave River. They were talking happily. Suddenly, Feng Qinqin tipped over a tree root and fell into the river. The river water was deep with torrent currents. Some people were fishing on the bank. All of them were in panic and didn't know what to do. Yingge took off his top immediately, threw away his shoes and jumped into the river. At this time, Feng Qinqin had been washed away for several meters. She shouted a bit and then nothing was heard. She was washed down by the torrent water. Yingge followed her and stretched his hand to reach Feng Qinqin but he couldn't do that. He just went down with the flow. Feng Qinqin happened to be stopped by the branches of a fallen tree caused by the wind. She was in a coma. Yingge grabbed her and dragged her to the bank. However, the currents were so rapid that he tried several times but failed. The waves beat against Yingge's face. It hurt. Yingge was going to collapse because of the water. Fortunately, two guys came to their rescue. One grabbed the big tree and another held Yingge's hand. Yingge held Feng Qinqin's hand tightly. In this way, the four of them came to the bank, hand in hand. Yingge thought at that time, no matter how dangerous it was, he would save Feng Qinqin. If his hand got loose, Feng Qinqin would be washed away by the river water. Therefore, he held her even if it would take his life. They would die together!

Yingge had to carried it through and finally risked his life of pulling little Feng to the bank in the end.

Feng Qinqin remained unconscious because she choked plenty of water. Yingge was motionless there, felt completely weak and was breathing heavily. Out of no reason, a blast of miraculous strength made Yingge wake up suddenly. He shouted, "Quick, save Feng Qinqin." The two young people were confused there and didn't know how to save her. Yingge said, "I will lay on my stomach. Pull Little Feng onto my back and let her head face downwards so as to empty the water in her belly. You beat her back and shake her full body. Then the water will be emptied. This is what I heard from the old people. Quick. Do what I said. Otherwise, she will die." Yingge lay on his stomach and limbs stretched. Little Feng was on his back. The two young men patted Little Feng's back, shook her thigh and pushed them forward. Indeed, lots of water came out of Little Feng's mouth and nose. The water could fill almost half the basin. Yingge couldn't hold up with the pressure on his back. At this time, Feng Qinqin woke up, "Oh, God!" She screamed, opened her eyes and finally came to her consciousness. Feng Qinqin ran towards Yingge and cried, "You saved me again. How come you are like this? You always save others in face of death. Don't you care about yourself!......" Yingge said, "I care, care, care...... As long as you are alive, everything is fine. Otherwise, how will I explain to your mother if anything happens to you? It's really fortunate." People of the bureau and the locomotive depot came. Little Ma borrowed a bicycle and helped Feng Qinqin onto the bike. Liu Cheng controlled the bike and sent her home.

10. Time Is Squeezed

Yingge had driving tasks to perform in order to carry wood from the mountains. Before every task, Yingge always put the books in his bag so that he could read the books anytime in spare time after going to mountains. He wanted to found time for learning and reading books whenever he was free.

After driving to the lumber storage yard and checking the train and all spare parts, Yingge thought there's no problem but he was still worried and let the assistant driver examine it again so as to ensure absolute safety in the operation. After that, he left the train and walked into the forest with his bag. He took a knife with him and walked to the left side of the big tree trunk ahead. He had a cut on the tree every a dozen of steps to leave a mark until he saw a comfortable place under a tree. He stopped and looked around. Then he climbed onto a tree and sat on the branch. After he's set, he started reading the book. It's safe to read on the tree because first it could prevent wild boars and wolves from biting you, and second it could avoid the attack of the serpent. It's getting dark. Birds started chirping and owls started hooting as if they were telling Yingge: stop reading, get off the tree and go home! It's too dangerous in the night. Seeing it's getting dark and hearing the sound of the birds, Yingge thought it's time to go home! Yingge heard lots of echoes and sounds, together with the blowing night wind, formed a horrible symphony. The night view in the forest was both mysterious and thrilling. Yingge got off the tree and headed back along the marks he made previously. This was a life experience in the forest area. If you didn't cut marks on the tree, you would be lost in the forest and might not be able to come out of it. Then it would be too dangerous. There had been many such examples in the past. The forest surveyors entered the depths of the mountains for measurement. At the beginning, they didn't have experience and didn't have technicians guide the way for them. They got lost in the depths and couldn't find the way back. In the end, they died in the virgin forest. At that time, there's no advanced communications equipment so access to the outside world was impossible and they couldn't be saved. The experience had been earned by lives. When you were walking the dense forest, you needed to make marks so that you could find the correct way.

As the sun set in the west and the moon rose out of the east, it's getting late and Yingge hadn't come back. People at home were so worried that they searched for Yingge everywhere. The leader of the forest farm was anxious as well and afraid that something bad happened to him. A group of people entered the forest and shouted with the accompaniment of gongs and drums which echoed in the forest. Little Feng yelled, "Our Yingge Dache, where are you? Where are you reading the book? Did you run into wolves or are you injured by serpents? We are here to help you!"

Hearing people's shouts, gongs and drums, Yingge followed the sound and finally met with them. Yingge was so moved and kept saying "thank you". He, together with others, went back to the lumber storage yard along the way they came. Feng Qinqin held Yingge's hand and walked with the rest of them with smile on her face. She's ready to return to the forest farm and the locomotive depot next day by taking the train.

The forest farm leader asked him, "Where have you been? Everyone is worried about you." Yingge answered, "I was reading in the forest. Unconsciously it's getting dark. After hearing people's shouts, I find them and come back with them."

Factory director Liu said, "Comrade Yingge, we admire your spirit of studying hard. You are already a technical college graduate but you are still learning new things and paid so much attention to it. What about us?"

Yingge said, "Talents with great knowledge are needed if our country is going to develop, proceed and move forward. Our current knowledge is not enough. We can't just be confined to the present; instead, we need to think about our future. The society is constantly developing. We can't just depend on physical work. Look at our workers. How tired they are! They are engaged in physical labor only. In future, if the wood is mechanically and automatically transported, and piling, un-piling as well as loading are conducted in the same way, lots of human labor will be saved. It's both fast and safe. Hence, we need to study hard, build our brain with science and technology, and handle production and transportation with scientific methods. It won't be long before we get to the era. It is coming soon."

11. Scrap Iron or Steel

Since last time when Yingge was criticized by Hu Erpao for going sign up for the college entrance exam, he had felt blue recently. He failed to sign up. What's worse, he was blamed and almost fired. Would he be able to go to college in future? With these conflicts on his mind, he was frustrated. It's a day off work. Liu Cheng came to talk with Yingge and noticed something was wrong with Yingge. He asked, "Yingge, what happened to you? Why are you unhappy?" Yingge answered, "I won't take the exam next year. Our leader and colleagues are not satisfied with it because they have limited cognition of college. I may as well work in the forest area in the rest of my life. I think it's quite good here with ample scope for my abilities." Liu Cheng said, "We are still young and we need to dream something. Man struggles upwards; water flows downwards." The two of them talked for a while and nobody was convinced.

Yingge walked into the forest alone. Still he had a knife in his hand and left cut marks on the trees while walking. He's humming and moved aimlessly. He stopped under a big tree and cut the name of Feng Qinqin on the trunk. It seemed that only Feng Qinqin could understand his "depression".

Oh, stars in the sky! Grass on the ground,
Who knows my frustration?
It's burning on my inner side,
Whom should I tell my frustration?
The big tree is with me along the way,
You have to make a decision.
You can't jump far,
And you can't fly high.
When will you be able to spread your wings?

And fly into the vast sky!

Stars! My destiny! I want to sing. Who can stop me from singing......

Yingge sung his morose song while walking. He missed Feng Qinqin more when he's down, "Little Feng, where are you! You know, I love you so much. It's love which bonds us together. I am praying to God that we will never part with each other."

There was no story without coincidences. Little Feng happened to come across Liu Cheng and she asked, "How's Yingge doing? Where's he?" Liu Cheng said, "He's sad these days. He doesn't want to study anymore and wants to give up the exam." Little Feng was extremely shocked and rapidly ran towards the forest which Yingge frequented. She followed the marks Yingge made and walked into the depths of the forest. She ran and shouted, "Yingge.....Where are you......". The trees were too dense here with lots of echoes. As she walked, she saw Yingge who was still indulged in his melancholy song. Feng Qinqin stood motionless under the tree and listened to Yingge. After he finished, Feng Qinqin rushed at him, "What's wrong with you, Yingge? Tell me. What's on your mind? Why are you alone here?" Yingge said, "Nothing special. I just want to have a little walk. I don't work today so I have time." Feng Qinqin asked, "Why don't you read your book and prepare for the exam?" Yingge said to her with emotions, "I don't want to take the exam now. Conditions don't allow it. I plan to spend the rest of my life with you in the forest area." "What?" Feng Qinqin was taken aback and asked, "You are not going to take the exam? Spend the rest of your life with me here?"

Feng Qinqin stared at Yingge angrily and tears coursed down her cheeks, "I have long looked forward to your success in the college entrance exam but I didn't think you would change. You are a person without ideal and prospect. You let me down. You will only beat yourself if you keep doing this....." Feng Qinqin was getting more and more agitated, "I have been taking you as my hero, my idol, model, my sweetheart and most admirable person. But now you are nothing but scrap iron!" The bitter denouncement made Yingge stupefied and dizzy. He didn't wake up until a moment later. Feng Qinqin suddenly turned into so bad-tempered from a kind and gentle girl. Yingge glared at her without a move as if he was a kid who just made a mistake. Feng Qinqin turned sad instead of angry. She became softhearted, hugged Yingge and cried with pain, "Forgive my anger. I hate you because I love you so much. If you don't take the exam with no ambition at all, don't see me anymore." Little Feng walked away without looking back. Yinggge shouted desperately, "Come back, little Feng! I need to talk to you." She walked out of the forest without looking back.

Yingge looked at Feng Qinqin's back and stayed still, saying to himself, "I am a piece of scrap iron. I am a piece of useless scrap iron? No! I am not! I am steel! Steel! I am the steel which is needed by the country and people. I am not scrap iron!" Yingge left the forest and went back to the dorm. Covered in the quilt, he tossed and turned on his grass bed, and couldn't fall asleep. Yingge rose and went to the dorm of Feng Qinqin. He indeed loved her and they were a love couple of life and death. After crossing over the little hill, Yingge went to the dorm of Feng Qinqin.

Yingge stood outside and through the window he saw Feng Qinqin was lying on her bed alone in night clothes and hummed melancholy,

Wind, wind, blow lightly,
Trees and leaves, shake slowly,
Who are you whispering about?
Wind, wind, blow lightly,
Please send a message for me.
I have something to say to Yingge,
Enthusiastic life depends on fighting.
Who's the love of Qinqin?
No one else but Yingge.
You are my soul. You are my heart.

You are my sweetheart.

Fish can't live without water. Melons can't live without seedlings.

Birds can't fly without wings. Green vines tangles around the tree while flowers love the sun.

Young men can't live without beautiful good girls.

Oh, wind! When can you deliver my message?

Hopefully Yinggge return to me soon.

It's going to be dawn. He's coming.

Come! I am waiting for you in the dream.

Come! I am your sweetheart.

As she was singing, she fell into sleep unconsciously. Qinqin's room door was unlatched. Yingge pushed the door quietly and came to her bed. With her graceful body, she was just like the fairy girl who came to the secular world. Her tiring face revealed pure beauty of women. She looked so charming that Yingge didn't want to wake her up. He sat beside the bed and it seemed that he was appreciating the best art model. In the serene evening, Yingge looked at Qinqin as if ancient heroes were attached to beauties. It's a lucky thing that you had sweet love to enjoy in your life. Yingge couldn't help touching the tender hands of Qinqin who finally woke up. Seeing it's Yingge, she hugged him immediately. It seemed that they were a couple who reunited after a long separation. After a burst of kisses, they hugged each other. Feng Qinqin, like flowers in full bloom, couldn't restrain herself. She pressed Yingge on the bed and went beyond herself. She was caressing and kissing. She wanted to let Yingge make love with her but she's shy to speak it out. In such an evening when nobody knew it and in the room where stars couldn't be seen, such charming moment shouldn't be missed. The blood of Yingge was boiling. The blooming flower was in front of him, his sweetheart……

Although Yingge was infatuated, he was suddenly awakened like being electronically shocked. He thought to himself: I can't, I can't. I need to control myself. Calm down. It's a test of scrap iron or steel. I have a long way to go. It could only bring about temporary happiness but it may bring her trauma in future. We are friends. I need to think about more. Yingge got off the bed calmly and kissed Feng Qinqin on her face with profound emotion. Then he said goodbye to her……

Feng Qinqin admired Yingge more: I am bent on marrying him. He's a person with great ideal and steel-like willpower. He's a steady-going man. He's an uncommonly great person in front of women……

12. Yingge Went to College and the Flames Were Ignited Again

The secretary of the locomotive depot came to look for Yingge and told him Secretary Li wanted to see him. Yingge said, "I am coming after I tidied up the train." After a short while, Yingge went to see Secretary Li with confusion. Just as he entered the room, Secretary Li told Yingge happily, "Good news! Your dream is going to come true. In order to train more personnel and encourage excellent young men with achievements and knowledge to go to college for further study, and with the discussion of the bureau, the locomotive depot recommends you to take the national college entrance exam this year. You must be excited, I think! From now on, you will spend time in preparing for it and review what you have learned before the exam. Wish you a success!"

Yingge was definitely happy and went up to hold Secretary Li's hands, "Thank you for your support, Secretary. I will be fully prepared for the exam as I am asked to. This year, there are lots of transportation tasks. Besides, I need to lecture for young drivers, write the book, evaluate and instruct on site. Although there's little time to study, I will try my best to lose no time to prepare for that."

Yingge left Secretary Li and went back to the dorm immediately. He started working hard. He used any available time to learn, recite and do exercises from early morning to the evening.

He often went to the forest with an oil lamp in the night. He studied both day and night, and almost forgot food and sleep. He's really bent on passing the exam and becoming useful to the country. After hearing that he's going to sign up for the exam, Feng Qinqin was especially happy and offered to wash clothes, sewed clothes and socks for him. Even she bought exercise books for him and did some other work that she could do so that Yingge could have more time to study.

With the approval of the bureau leader, 18 excellent high school graduates, secondary technical school and technical college graduates were chosen to take the exam on behalf of 12,000 employees of the bureau. The locomotive depot had over 900 employees at present. Only Yingge and Liu Cheng were selected. However, it's not bad according to the ratio.

It's the exam date on July 25. A month was left before the exam. Yingge was stressed but he's fully confident and went all out to prepare for the exam.

God help those who help themselves. The date of August 25, 1954, was the day which Yingge would never forget. On that day, Secretary Li asked someone to call Yingge to his office. Seeing Yingge, Secretary Li smiled, "Congratulations! Congratulations! You succeed. The college letter of admission has been delivered to the general bureau. You are admitted by Heilongjiang University. Finally one of us passes the exam. You are awesome. What an honor for our bureau and our depot. There are over 20 institutions in the entire bureau. Only you passed the exam. Other institutions speak highly of us now. We must celebrate for your going to college."

It's just in time! It's the first time that the locomotive depot had a college student. Yingge said to himself, "You need to work harder! Don't fail the Party and people. You need to be the pillar of your motherland and contribute to its construction. Try to have further studies in the Soviet Union after college."

Yingge declared to Secretary Li, "Secretary Li, I will study hard. After graduation, I will return to contribute to our locomotive depot, build our locomotive depot with science and technology and let it be mechanical, electrified and automatic. Besides, it will have new trains."

"Okay! Welcome to come back after graduation." said Secretary Li.

On September 1, new term began. The general bureau held a farewell party on August 28. On that day, it's sunny and the autumn wind blows gently. Over a hundred of people gathered on the platform and saw Yingge off. Feng Qinqin was the most hospitable one. She helped Yingge carry his luggage and ran around. The drums and gongs team and Yangko dance team of the general bureau had a performance. It's as boisterous as New Year. Director General Yuan of the general bureau got off the jeep. Yingge went forward, held his hands tightly and wept even before he could speak.

The director general made a loud speech in front of the crowd, "Dear comrades! What a joyful moment! Our bureau's advanced worker comrade Yingge has passed the exam and is admitted by a famous university. Heilongjiang University is one of the well-known universities in the Northeast China and even the entire country. It's no easy job to be admitted to this university among so many students in the country. It means that comrade Yingge has an ideal and is capable of outstanding achievements. We need to learn from him. We need to reward him. On behalf of the general bureau, I will give RMB 500 to him for reward so that he can go to college with payment. That's how we support comrade Yingge. How about it?" Applause and cheers were heard on site and the siren of the train reverberated. Yingge was going to get on the train. Suddenly, Feng Qinqin crossed the crowd and came up with a bouquet of flowers in her hand. She handed it to Yingge affectionately and gave him a bag in which it's a notebook and a sweater which she weaved herself. Feng Qinqin stood in front of Yingge with both happiness and enthusiasm. She wanted to hug and kiss him but she restrained herself in front of the crowd. Just like anyone else, she gave her regards and saw him get on the train with attachment and affection...... Yingge waved his hand through the window. Goodbye...... the virgin forest, Dahai Forestry Bureau, my leaders, my colleagues and my beloved......

Part III College Days

1. Farewell to the Black Land—Snowy Forest

In the train heading for Harbin, a myriad of thoughts crowded into his mind as the train was running. The past constantly occurred to him. In the endless Snowy Forest, Yingge had gradually become mature with four years' physical and mental training. In the past, he had fought against the poor life environment, beaten wild boars, wild wolves and tigers, and stood the ice snow and bitter coldness. Fortunately he survived. In the past few years, he had been devoted his work and performed driving tasks with diligence. With a pioneering spirit, he was engaged in reforms and inventions, thus becoming a technical backbone of the entire bureau. He had created a legendary life on his life journey which could be regarded as a great wealth of his life. It meant that in future Yingge would face different difficulties, hardships and challenges with more solid foundations, and start his fiery college days with vigorous steps.

Yingge was a person of feelings who knew to return others' favor. Although he's going to college, he wouldn't forget the late old classmates and comrades-in-arms who had fought, lived and got along with him. They would sleep here forever in the depths of the forest where human traces were rare but they had contributed to the development of the motherland's forestry cause. Out of luck, Yingge was still alive but he also brushed past the Death God before.

Before leaving the black land, Yingge went to the tomb again to say goodbye with tears in his eyes. He bowed for three times in front of his comrades-in-arms' graves, kneed down and presented the mountain flowers he picked. They were: Zhang Jincheng, Guo Yongqing, Li Weimin and Zhao Qingshan, etc. All of them were Yingge's good classmates and good comrades-in-arms. They sacrificed with honor in the fulfillment of their tasks. Some of them died of train crash against mountain creeks due to deviation from the trails; some of them were bit to death by wild boars while stopping the train and repairing it. They contributed their young lives for the construction of their motherland.

Zhang Jincheng was two years elder than Yingge. Yingge called him Elder Brother and he called Yingge Younger Brother. They got well along with each other. They often went to the mountains to pick wild fruits, mushrooms and fungus on their days off. In daily life, Zhang Jincheng cared about Yingge in many aspects. Sometimes when the dining hall had some good dish, he would buy it and keep it for Yingge.

One day, Zhang Jincheng drove the train to carry wood for the kitchen and would come back in the afternoon. It's a day off but he voluntarily did that although it's unpaid. Therefore, Yingge went to the mountains alone to pick his favorite mountain strawberries so as to appreciate the service of Elder Brother Zhang Jincheng.

However, after picking wild fruits in the mountain forest, Yingge planned to go back but he was lost. He kept returning to the same place in the forest. He thought that he would be bit to death if he still couldn't walk out of the forest in the evening. He deeply knew that once you got lost in the forest, there's no way you could get out of it. There's nothing he could do. He sat there dejectedly. Misfortune was waiting for him……

Elder Brother Zhang drove the train back. He heard that Yingge went to the mountains to pick strawberries but still hadn't come back. He immediately realized that Yingge must get lost so he went into the mountains with a sharp axe and a color pencil. Whenever he came across a big tree, he would write a number on a small piece of tree skin. When the number reached 720, he finally saw his younger brother beside whom was a big basket of strawberries. He shouted happily, "Little brother!" Yingge raised his head to find his elder brother came to his rescue. He went up right away, "Oh, my dear brother! If you don't come, I would have died here." Yingge was so moved that he wept……

They cut off a stick to carry the strawberries and then they walked out of the dense forest by following the marks on the tree.

Yingge recalled the incident. That year, he stood in front of the tomb and said to himself, "I would have been killed in the mountains but for the timely help of Elder Brother Zhang. Today I am still alive. How can I forget my savior? Dear comrades-in-arms, may you rest at peace! As long as I am alive, I will work hard and fight! Climb! I will finish what you haven't completed." Yingge kneed down before the tomb with a myriad of thoughts on his mind, "One's life is limited. When you are still alive, you need to lose no time to fight because nobody knows when you will be beat by misfortune or cruel diseases. Then you won't stand on your feet and there's no opportunity to fight. Since you are alive, you should take the opportunity to climb and cherish precious time to contribute to your motherland……!"

Yingge stood up and bowed again to his comrades-in-arms with affection: Dear comrades-in-arms, goodbye! I am leaving you to go to college. I am going to live in new environment. I am not going to live in ease and comfort but to face new challenges. I will study science and technology hard and surpass new peaks of science so as to build our great motherland. He wiped out his tears and walked back, leaving the "footprint" of reluctance to separate before the tomb of his comrades-in-arms.

2. New Challenge

Yingge came to Heilongjiang University, one of the well-known universities in the country, with building of European styles. It's built according to the drawing of Moscow State University. It's both magnificent and solemn. The beautiful campus deeply attracted Yingge, his desire for knowledge and his young and enthusiastic heart. With full confidence, he faced his new life and challenges.

Tall buildings, clean classrooms and verdant pines cypresses made him feel like he's living in a wonderland and stand in awe for the northern institution of higher learning. He would study for five years and spend his fiery college days here. There were also European, African, Asian and Latin American students here.

However, in the preparatory test after entrance, his foreign language performance was not good due to poor foundation. It meant that in future study he needed to work harder and made greater efforts than others if he wanted to catch up with others. Severe challenges and difficulties were ahead. If he failed the exam, he would have to go back to the lower level or be forced to drop out. How terrible the consequences were!

Facts proved that Yingge was indeed a person who worked hard and didn't fear hardships. After 21:00, the lights on campus were turned off and there's no place for study. Only the lights in the toilets were still on. With those lights, he memorized Russian words. Yingge was short-tempered and aggressive. He desired to excel over others in study. At many nights when he recited Russian texts in the toilet, he tried to memorize them for several times and actually fell into sleep in the end due to tiredness. He hated himself after opening his eyes: How can I catch up with others if I do like this? He slapped himself as punishment. He shouted while slapping himself, "How can you catch up with others with your level? Why are you so stupid and can't memorize it! Who asks you to sleep......" He was not lenient to himself at all. He slapped so hard that the sound could be heard...... There's only one wall between women's toilet and men's toilet. Hearing the sound and shouts in the men's toilet at night, girls in the toilet thought boys were having a fight in the toilet so they reported to the security office of the university. Two guards from the office went to the men's toilet with their torchlight. They stood outside and listened for a while. They entered to see that only Yingge was learning Russian and reading the book quietly. They asked Yingge, "Did you notice someone fight here just now?" Yingge said, "No. Only me. I have been reading a book here." "Then why did girls hear slapping sounds and shouts in men's toilet?" Yingge felt embarrassed and explained with a smile on his face, "The girl misunderstood. I slapped myself because I couldn't memorize those Russian words. Just look at my face."

The two guards laughed and admired Yingge's hard-working spirit. They looked at their watch, "It's over 1:00 o'clock. Go back to your dorm and sleep! You need to go to class tomorrow." Then Yingge went back to his dorm. He spent his college days like this. Work hard, harder and harder! Study, study and study! Constant effort yields sure success, which was an ancient saying.

With his efforts, he eventually overcame difficulties in Russian words and grammar. Next he needed to improve his speaking and listening. Teachers were foreign ones who didn't speak Chinese. Yingge was often criticized for his poor Russian competence. It's very important to improve his speaking and listening in order to understand foreign teachers in class. He couldn't find a way out, "I am physically tall. What's the use? But now I am indeed inferior to others in Russian. What should I do?" Who's Yingge? He's someone who couldn't be beaten by difficulties and was good at using his brain. With deep consideration, he finally came up with a method. After class, Yingge went to talk with foreigners to practice Russian. In order to have more contacts with foreigners, he found opportunities to make friends with foreigners and visit foreigners in their houses. Every Sunday he went to the foreign church, kneed down and attended the religious service. He didn't believe in God. He went there only to practice his listening and talk with foreigners by the way. Hard work paid off. Several years later, his speaking and listening were constantly improved. He could chat and discuss with foreigners. He could speak fluently with his foreign teacher in class. His speaking was the best in the class and he even served as the subject representative.

3. Donate Blood to Save People

It's silent at night. It's 22:50. Yingge was alone and was reading in the toilet with the lights. Suddenly somebody shouted and asked students to get up and go to the affiliated hospital to donate blood. A patient needed to be saved. Yingge was the first one coming out of the toilet. He asked about details and went to the dorm to wake up his classmates. Then he led a dozen of classmates to the hospital and wait for blood donation. He's familiar with the way to Heilongjiang University Hospital.

It turned out that an overseas student from "Zimbabwe" of Africa suffered from acute peritonitis and needed a surgery. Huge blood transfusion was demanded to save him. Yingge said the African person was the friend of Chinese people and alumnus of Heilongjiang University so they had to try their best to save him. The doctor said, "The student is quite tough. He contacted appendicitis at the beginning but he needed to study. Therefore, he didn't come to the hospital for treatment in time. After it's festered, the disease was evolved into acute peritonitis. Over a meter of the small intestine is worn out and needs to be removed. He can't be saved if it's a bit late. The timing of those classmates who come to donate their blood is perfect."

In that backward era, people were worried about blood donation and fell short of sufficient cognition of blood drawing. Although classmates were here, nobody dared to be the first one. After repeated persuasion of the doctor, each of them agreed to contribute 50CC. When the nurse came to ask their blood type, Yingge stood in the front and asked the doctor what the maximum amount he could contribute if he didn't want to affect his study. The doctor said 200CC. Yingge rolled up his sleeve, "Come! I will be the first and I want to contribute 300CC. It's urgent to save him." After Yingge was done, he drank a glass of hot water and lay on the bed for rest. Each of other classmates contributed 50CC. They totally donated 1,500CC and then left. The surgery was not a small one. 1.5 meters of small intestine was removed. The blood was used up but the surgery was not done yet. 400CC was still missing. There's not enough time to get people. However, if the blood was not ready, all previous efforts were wasted. At this time, Yingge resolutely stretched his arm and asked the doctor to draw 400CC more. Yingge's indomitable spirit touched the doctor and nurse. They said: 200CC will do! You have already donated enough. The rest 200CC will be donated by us. With concerted efforts, an international move of healing the wounded and rescuing the dying was adopted. In the end, the international friend, the alumnus of Heilongjiang University and our black brother was saved. The surgery was quite successful with common efforts of medical staff.

Chairman Mao's inscription hang on the wall of the hospital, "Heal the wounded and rescue the dying was adopted; implement revolutionary humanism."

Yingge went back to the university. The instructor asked him not to take the class and go back for a rest because he donated too much blood. However, Yingge went to the class in the afternoon. He's afraid that he might not be able to catch up if he didn't take the class. He's persistent and was reluctant to rest for the sake of study. In the third afternoon class, he couldn't hold on anymore. He felt fainted and fell onto the ground. Classmates sent him to the infirmary immediately. He finally came to his consciousness after urgent rescue. Even so, he still cared about how the black classmate was going in the hospital. The doctor criticized the instructor that he shouldn't let him donate so much blood. It's too dangerous. He needed to rest and eat nutritious food.

4. Learn Russian in the Big Church

With great efforts, Yingge's Russian level was improved soon. He could follow the teacher in class but his speaking and listening were still not desirable. Hence, he wanted to communicate with Russian people. He must be brave to ask questions and talk with Russian people in order to improve his Russian. Surely he needed to be very polite to them. Only in this way could he improve his speaking and listening.

Once he took the bus to Jesus Church of Russian people and listen to the archbishop who lectured the Holy Bible. Yingge offered his seat to an old Russian woman and took the opportunity to talk with her. He asked in Russian where she was heading, which street she lived and what families she had, what did she do, what she was up to in senior life, what she learned when she was young, how her life was and whether her home was cold or not in winter...... The old Russian woman answered his questions in Russian. Yingge sincerely asked, “Do you have any difficulty? Do you need my help? What can I do for you?” The old woman was considerably moved.

They were so happy and reached the destination unconsciously. She’s going to get off. Yingge realized he missed his stop because he’s just engaged in talking with the old lady. He had to take the bus back. After two stops, he came to the Jesus Church.

It’s too cold in winter in the north. The ground was covered with ice. An old Russian woman was walking towards the church with difficulty. Yingge trotted forward to help her to the church. The old woman went there to pray to God while Yingge was there to learn Russian. He and the old woman kneed down on the ground to listen to the archbishop who was reading the Holy Bible. It’s too tiring to knee down for the whole morning to listen to the archbishop while speaking Russian and chatting with the old lady. Nonetheless, he’s happy because his listening was greatly improved.

Before in class, the female foreign teacher asked him a question. He didn’t get it and only answered with one sentence. The teacher was so angry that she stamped with fury and reported to the instructor, saying that Yingge “insulted her” in class. At that time, Yingge even didn’t know what happened.

The teacher's question in class was, "What do the little hens we raise at home provide for us every day?" The simple answer was: little hens lay eggs for us every day. However, Yingge didn't give this answer. He forgot the Russian word and mixed it with another word. His answer was: little hens lay "female teachers" every day. It enraged the teacher. How come the hens lay female teachers?! "Nonsense. You are stupid and idiot......" The teacher stared at Yingge and was furious. Yingge made a stupid mistake. Later, he apologized to the teacher and begged her to forgive him. It really influenced Yingge. He was determined and swore to overcome Russian language.

At that time, Yingge kept thinking about a word. He just couldn't memorize it so even in class, he kept saying pelienadaowalaca (female teacher) and pumice (hen). The last syllable of the word "female teacher" sounded almost the same with the last syllable of the word "hen". Therefore, Yingge mistook the word "female teacher" for "hen". He should answer "lay eggs" but he said "hens can lay female teachers", which was a ridiculous joke and misunderstanding. Yingge was really affected by the incident. Later, he apologized to the female teacher and asked her to forgive him!

Since then, Yingge had deeply realized that he must understand the meaning of foreigners first while strengthening his listening and speaking training. He should answer after knowing what the question meant.

In addition to more listening and speaking practices in class, he spared some time to have access to foreigners and make friends with them. He even went to their houses. At the beginning, he didn't know their etiquette so they were angry and drove him off. After many times of consultation, he knew the etiquette of contacting with foreigners. Later on, it got smooth when he conducted verbal communication with them. His foreign language level was improved soon.

Yingge kneed down in the church to listen to the Holy Bible lecture for a long time in Jesus Church. The concrete floor was ice cold and there's no cushion on the floor. His legs couldn't stand for so long time. His knee joints suffered from inflammation due to coldness. His legs were so painful that he couldn't stand up. Once, in the church, Yingge spoke loud and was heard by the archbishop. The archbishop came in front of Yingge and spoke in Russian, "Who are you? What are you doing here? You speak so loud. Get out!" He grabbed Yingge's ear and pulled him. Yingge shook off his hand and shouted in Russian, "Moiré Bok, oh, my God! Save me please. I am the loyal son of God. I want to learn the Holy Bible but someone doesn't let me. The archbishop was driving me away." Yingge's yelling in Russian really shocked the archbishop-- the Father. He dared not drive Yingge. The efforts Yingge made in learning Russian were several times greater than others and even dozens of times greater. As the old saying went, real knowledge came from practice. It could be steeled in repeated struggles. He said, " If you work at it hard enough, you can grind an iron rod into a needle." Yingge's indomitable spirit of learning moved the teacher and God. He started with letters and leaped to one of the best students in the class. He was selected as excellent learning student by classmates in the class. According to him, one couldn't make achievements in learning language if he's lazy. Language depended on practice and speaking. It's even forced. In order not to let down the motherland, he studied harder and harder, practice more and more, and made greater and greater efforts. Just as Marx said, "There is no royal road to science, and only those who do not dread the fatiguing climb of its steep paths have a chance of gaining its luminous summits." Yingge manifested the truth with his actions.

Since then, Yingge had left the footprint of studying Russia hard in the university.

5. Prepare for Preparatory Graduation Exam

Yingge worked hard with arduous and phenomenal efforts. He had paid huge price which ordinary people could hardly imagine and completed the preparatory study with extraordinary performance. The preparatory courses were taught by Chinese and foreign teachers. Regular college courses were lectured by foreigners. Therefore, if one couldn't graduate from the preparatory study, he wouldn't catch up in regular college courses.

There were three deployed students in Yingge's class. One of them couldn't follow the schedule and had to drop out and return to his original institution. Another failed the exam so he had to study all over again. This was the last chance.

The preparatory graduation exam was coming. Yingge worked hard in daily time so he had an ace up his sleeve about the exam. He's not so worried about it but he's a bit nervous.

Thinking of this, Yingge wanted to know whether his exam results would be good or not.

The exam day finally came. First it's oral exam which was the most difficult one. Few students could pass it.

The chief examiner professor stood before the blackboard. Those who were sitting in the examiners area included lecturers, university leaders, academic dean, professors and assistant postgraduates. The scene was extremely solemn. There were three students in the classroom. After drawing lots, the first student sat beside the little table in front of the teachers, and prepared for the questions and defense. The two remaining students sat behind the first student and prepared for the exam.

Yingge walked into the classroom calmly. The first got 3 marks with great difficulty; the second failed. It's Yingge's turn to defend. The first question the teacher asked, "What's your impression on Heilongjiang University since you have studied here for over a year? Please talk about it in Russian."

Yingge thought it's a big question and difficult to answer. Usually students didn't know where to start with the answer. However, Yingge understood the question and he thought about it for a little while. He answered in Russian, "Heilongjiang University is one of the well-known and comprehensive universities in the province and even the country. Professors in Heilongjiang University not only had profound and erudite knowledge but also were experienced in educating and teaching students. The university has many subjects such as literal arts, engineering, science, traffic, aviation and foreign languages. It's the cradle for training top high-tech personnel. The training goals and success roads of Heilongjiang University kept pace with and can be compared those famous international universities such as Harvard University and Yale University in U.S., Moscow State

University in the Soviet Union, Oxford University in Britain, University of Paris in France, University of Berlin in Germany, Tokyo University and Waseda University in Japan......"

The academic dean asked Yingge, "How do you evaluate your teachers?"

Yingge looked at Professor Anna and answered fluently in Russian, "In the past year of study in Heilongjiang University and with the evangelistic instructions of my teachers, I have made great progress. At the beginning, I could only speak several words. Today, I can stand here to answer your question. It's a great leap. All of this results from teachers' efforts. Surely it's inseparable from the university's training and my own efforts. Here, I would like to extend my gratitude to the university leaders for their training. Thank you!" Yingge bowed with affection and won the teachers' warm applause.

Professor Anna asked in Russian, "What do you think of learning Russian? Why do you like Russian?"

Yingge answered after thinking for a while, "A foreign language is just like a bridge to the outside world and a boat which leads to the other side of the ocean. A bridge is a must to cross the river and there's no way of crossing the ocean without a boat. Therefore, in order to exchange technologies with the outside world and spread friendship, the grasp of a foreign language is a must. A foreign language is a key to the world's window."

Yingge answered, "I learn Russian and love Russian because Russian is the language of the great Russian nation. Russia is the hometown of the grand October Revolution and the first socialist country led by Lenin. Besides, it's the flag of the world's revolutions. There are heroic people, strong national defense and advanced science and technology in the country. I love Russia. Marx even studied Russian when he was 51 years old. Languages of different nations have different features. Just as the greatest scientist of Russia Lomonosov said, Russia possesses the fortitude of Germany, sentiment and gentleness of French, unrestraint of

Slavic, concise power and emotional expression of Greek, the brightness and magnificence of Spanish." His answer won another burst of warm applause.

Professor Liu of the exam committee posed another question, "How do you learn Russian?"

As to this question, Yingge had lots of feelings because his study had been hard and painstaking.

Yingge continued, "In my experience, it's not difficult to learn a language but it's hard to be proficient at it. Painstaking efforts and brain work are required. There's no way that you can excel at a foreign language if you don't make great efforts, learn widely from others' strong points and pursue excellence. I am a case in point. If I didn't study harder and harder with indomitable perseverance in daily time, I wouldn't have been able to stand here to answer your questions."

Doctor Jiang, the academic dean of the university asked in Russian, "What Russian works have you read? Which one is your favorite? Why?"

Yingge said, "My study schedule is tight in the university so I don't have too much time in reading too many extracurricular books. In future I will reader more Russian books. What I have read include Lev Tolstoy's *War and Peace, Resurrection* and *Collection of Nekrasov's Poems*, etc."

Assistant postgraduate asked, "What else have you read?"

Yingge said, "During my study here, I have read works of some Russian writers such as Chernyshevsky's *What To Do*, Sholodhov's *And Quiet Flows the Don*, the poet Pushkin's *Eugene Onegin*, *Collection of Lermontov's Poems* and *Collection of Mayakovsky's Poems* as well as the Soviet Union literature works such as Gorky's trilogy *Mother*, *Childhood* and *My Universities*, *Far from Moscow*, Simonov's *Day and Night*, Ostrovsky's *How the Steel Was Tempered*, etc."

The Doctor continued, "Do you like *How the Steel Was Tempered*?"

Yingge answered, "Yes, I like it."

Professor Anna seemed interested, "Why do you like it?"

Yingge answered in Russian, "I like the protagonist Paul • Korchagin who is the hero of the Soviet Union people and young men as well. His words have always encouraged me and I regard him as a good example of mine." He paused for a while and affectionately recited the famous remark in the book which almost all young people can recite, 'It is of course life that human should cherish most. Everyone has only one life, and it should be spent like this. When one memorizes and looks back to what he has experienced, he wouldn't regret for the precious years he wasted, and he wouldn't either be shamed for living in idleness and achieving nothing. At the moment he is going to die, he is eligible to say: the whole of my life and effort have both been devoted to the most grateful career in the history that is to fight for freedom of human beings.'" Teachers and students applauded again.

His powerful intonation and passion from the bottom of his heart stunned those chief examiners. Yingge's performance was outstanding. The applause already reverberated through the entire room before his voice faded.

At this time, Yingge was no longer nervous about the exam; instead, he's more confident.

Yingge continued, "When you are alive, you should lose no time to study, live and fight. Quick! Take actions! You don't know when misfortune or sudden diseases will attack you and take away your lives. Then you collapse and won't be able to stand on your feet. You won't have opportunity to fight and work hard for your motherland." At this moment, lots of classmates outside the door were listening to Yingge. More and more classmates were gathering there and accidentally pushed the door open. They swarmed into the room.

The chief examiner said, "Come in, welcome! Now I hope all of you can hear Yingge's defense."

One assistant doctoral student asked, "You have read lots of poem collections. Which one do you like? Can you recite it in Russian?" Then a doctoral student chipped in, "Which poet do you like?"

Yingge said, "Mayakovsky."

The Doctor asked, "Can you recite his poem?"

Yingge said, "I love his long verse *Lenin* very much."

Yingge paused a bit and then recited loudly as if he were an actor with emotions:

In the dim sky with dense fog,

On the earth with turbulence,

On the vast sea with billowing waves,

Who is it pushes aside dark clouds to reveal the sunny blue sky?

Who is it prevents the rain and storm from beating the earth?

Who is it guides the boat to the other side of the sea?

It's Lenin, a great flag-bearer. It's Russia, the strength of great people.

Look at the sunny and bright sky,

Look at those rows of tall buildings. How splendid they are!

Towering in the sky. It's all mine! Do you know?

Also, look at the straight and wide Lenin Avenue where trees stand tall and flowers blossom. How beautiful it is!

It's also mine!

Look at the airplanes in the sky, vessels on the sea and trains running on the rails. Do you know?

They are also mine! Do you understand!!

Oh, motherland! You are my mother! I am your son!

Oh, motherland! Let them watch! Let them be jealous! Let them admire! It's all mine. How rich I am! Let them envy!

I am a citizen of the great Russia! My dear motherland! My heart is bonded with yours!

All people in the classroom were listening quietly. They got excited, cheered and applauded him. Professor Anna, the Russian teacher, went up to Yingge with tears in her eyes. She couldn't speak for a long while, hugged her excellent student with enthusiasm and cried with emotions. Little did she think a student who was poor at Russian in the class and could only tell few words could actually become the most outstanding student in the class and even the entire grade. The female teacher's face is permeated with pride and glory.

She finally cried out: **Харощо** (Well done). The teacher examiners including assistant postgraduates happened to coincide to give the highest mark—five. People in the room rose and clapped their hands for a long while. Yingge, amid crowded classmates, went out of the room. They carried him and tossed him upwards. They were passionate, joyful and cheerful: Yingge did a great job. A great job!!

6. We Need to Be Down to Earth

Yingge got famous for his excellent performance in the preparatory exam so he enjoyed great credibility among his classmates. They unanimously elected him as the League branch secretary and let him to guide them for regular college courses.

Yingge had advanced ideologies and studied hard. He's the example for other students. He wanted to join in the Communist Party and become a glorious member so much. It's the goal of all progressive young people. Yingge among all students was a League member and the first one to submit the Party membership application. It's Yingge's political goal to study hard for the construction of the motherland and be dedicated to the communist cause during his study in Heilongjiang University.

One day, Yingge went to the political section of the university to attend a political report mobilization meeting. His mood became especially heavy after returning to the class and he didn't know how to deliver what's said in the meeting to the entire class. He didn't know how to carry it out in the class. He felt frustrated, restless and worried. Out of normal behaviors, he was not himself anymore. The spirit of the meeting was that whether a student was rich or poor, revolutionary or counterrevolutionary could be identified from his family background. The conclusion was: the poorer, the more revolutionary; the richer, the more counterrevolutionary.

After repeated consideration of the leader's speech, he guessed the general meaning was like this: students coming from poor and lower-middle peasant families were revolutionary while students from landlord and rich families were counterrevolutionary. It's a cruel political fight. They were wearing colored spectacles to look for the right-wings among young students, check their opinions, find their faults and seize counterrevolutionary ones. They were trying to take out all students with bad families background, titled them with rightists and asked other students to stay away from them. A cruel political storm disrupted the purity and serenity of the campus.

However, in the eyes of Yingge, all these students were vigorous young people and classmates. Some of them served as the heads of study departments and some the heads of entertainment and sports departments. Yingge just couldn't figure out why they had to be labeled as counterrevolutionary and discriminated overnight. He's extremely anguish which couldn't be described. Even if they looked down upon deployed students in the past and said Yingge was "old-fashioned", Yingge didn't want revenge. Even if he had the power to decide they were right-wings and counterrevolutionary students, and the organization trusted him, he couldn't just abuse the power.

Just as Yingge worked hard and was positively bent on becoming a member of the Party, the political storm which shocked all overseas Chinese swept around the country. In particular, colleges and universities were in the forefront of the issue. A cruel political storm destroyed the purity and serenity of the campus.

The objects of the campaign were mainly advanced intellectuals. Different people responded differently to the campaign. Some were wondering with confusion; some were terrified; some didn't care and some were dejected. Some contemptible scoundrels were anxious to see the world in disorder and made trouble everywhere in the name of the Party. What about Yingge? He didn't belong to any group. He was just so frustrated that he couldn't fall into sleep at night.

Yingge ruminated and just couldn't fathom it so he went to the political instructor for a talk who asked, "Yingge, what do you want to talk to me?"

Yingge said, "I am confused about something so I want to talk with you. Is it okay?"

The political instructor said, "Sure. Just tell me!"

"First, can one choose his family background? For example, a student likes poor and lower-middle peasants so would he be able to choose to be born in such families? He likes money so can he choose to be born in landlord and rich families. Is it?"

The instructor answered, "Of course not. People can't choose their birth families."

"Second, since it can't be chosen, are those students born in poor and lower-middle peasant families sure to be revolutionary? Are their heads marked with revolutionary symbols? Are their blood necessarily revolutionary blood? Must they be good people and revolutionaries?"

"Are the heads of students born in landlord and capitalist families marked with counterrevolutionary symbols? Are their blood counterrevolutionary blood? Must they be 'counterrevolutionaries' or not be revolutionaries?"

The instructor said, "No. Whether a person is revolutionary or not depends on himself and whether he receives the Party's education or not. Surely families have certain influences over them which, however, are not absolute. It mainly relies on his performance and his attitude towards revolution and socialist construction."

Yingge followed, "With the leadership of the Communist Party, the People's Republic of China has been established. The integration into the great cause of our motherland is the difference between revolutionary and anti-revolutionary people. People are revolutionary as long as they stand up for the Party, love socialist motherland, contribute their strength and talents to the construction cause, actively build our country, innovate, create and fight, give full scope to their talents and strength, aren't they? We should focus on their performances instead of their family background. If those who seize right-wings among young students are regarded as going with the trend and the Party with progressive ideologies and can be accepted by the Party, I would rather not to be a member. I don't want to do anything against my conscience. I don't want to feel guilty. Please forgive me. Instructor, I always think if a person is not righteous, he doesn't have a soul!"

According to the superior leader's instructions, three right-wings must be reported. Yingge felt lots of pressure at that time. He was the monitor in the class and had the right to report the profiles of the right-wings. If he could report three right-wings, he would finish his political task and even could be admitted to the Party. However, Yingge didn't know what to do and thought about it day and night. The more he thought, the more sad he was. He found it too cruel to report them.

The general information on the three "right-wings" were as follows:

I. One student whose family ran a grocery which sold oil, salt, tissue and daily supplies would be forcefully regarded as a little capitalist and right wing.

II. A clerk who worked as an accountant in a small workshop was regarded as a capitalist like "Huang Shiren" and counted as a right-wing.

III. One student whose father in the village who went to work in the city, became a worker later and then turned into a rich peasant was also regarded as a right-wing.

Yingge did not have the heart to divide the three classmates into the right-wing group. Although he could have finished the task assigned by the superior, he would have felt guilty. They didn't do anything bad and had nothing to do with right-wings. They were not against the Party and socialism. Moreover, they were good young men, heads of the study department, sports and entertainment departments. They usually responded to the call of the Party and support Yingge's work in an active way. The only thing was that they proposed their critical opinions about the Party branch in terms of work and teaching at one meeting, which caused disaster for them. Yingge thought: even if I didn't become a Party member, I wouldn't think divide them into right-wings and destroy them.

A Party member in the class reminded Yingge, "You are an activist of the Party application so you have to follow the superior instructions. No matter what you report, right or wrong, the anti-right-wing fight is the task assigned by the superior. You can't sympathize them; otherwise, it's not good to your Party application and yourself. Think about it. Think about the consequences."

He continued, "Li Lin laughed at you before. He said you were 'old-fashioned', had no training promise and would be expelled by the university sooner or later. Don't be polite to him. You can teach him a lesson and take him down."

Yingge didn't think so. For him, even if Li Lin teased him and despised him, he couldn't abuse his public power to retaliate against him. The right-wing title couldn't be given randomly because it would affect the future of one person in his lifetime who wouldn't be able to raise his head again. He abused me, looked down upon and slandered me. His performance was indeed poor at that time. He always failed the exam.

Yingge said, "The watershed and touchstone of real or false revolutionaries are dedication of their intelligence and talents to the socialist construction of their motherland. Right now, they haven't completed their study and don't have the opportunity to apply their talents out there in society and show their abilities. It's too early to divide them into counterrevolutionaries. It's unfair and hard to understand to treat them as bad people."

Yingge had a hunch that it might be difficult for him to be a Party member since he sympathized "right-wings". However, after a second thought, the most valuable about one person was his righteousness and down to earth spirit. Whether a person is a real or false revolutionary and a real or false Party member was determined by his lifetime contribution to his motherland and his lifetime fight for the Party's cause. It's better to leave it to the history for test!

Yingge's opinion was not wrong. However, under that kind of historical conditions, the realization of his dream of joining in the Party was indeed affected. However, he had nobody to blame. Who should shoulder the responsibility? Who would be responsible for his future? No one was there to answer his perplexity. Yingge was buried in extreme agony.

Yingge failed to have a "right" cognition of the anti-right-wing fight and his conscience didn't allow him to make false reports. His troubles and frustrations couldn't be described by words. He lost the opportunity to join in the Party. His study schedule was still tight. During that period, he had sleepless nights and wasn't in the mood of eating. He ended up falling ill. He went to the hospital and found he contacted the most terrible disease--tuberculosis. Oh, God, save Yingge!

His classmates went to the hospital to visit and comfort him on a regular basis. He couldn't stay in the hospital for too long because of his tight study schedule. He was discharged soon with his strong request.

7. The Art Show of Heilongjiang University Shocked the Entire City

Heilongjiang University had a galaxy of student talents. The annual art show provided a platform for these versatile students to show their capabilities. The art show of every year made students, teachers, university leader and even the municipal leaders happy. Student representatives of colleges and universities in the city came to appreciate the show. The joyful atmosphere was like New Year.

As the monitor, Yingge must be active. His class was going to graduate and he called on all classmates to present a gift to the university with their best excellent show.

Yingge's speech was quite humorous. He said, "Heilongjiang University has nurtured us for years. We are going to graduate but we have to return her. We must show our talents to our heart's content just as the eight immortals crossed the sea with their own techniques. It's time to show your real capability. We must work hard for our final art show! We need to give full scope to our strengths. We can only succeed. Dear classmates, are you confident?" They answered in unison, "Yes!"

With conscientious and painstaking rehearsals, they indeed worked out some exquisite programs. After careful screening, solo, dance and opera were selected as the major programs for the art show.

A pre-test was conducted. The first program was tenor and soprano duet by Yingge and Liu Qun: My Son, an Italian folk song sung in foreign language. Yingge had a solid foundation for singing. His voice was resonant and mellow. He cooperated with Liu Qun seamlessly with one climax after another. The program shocked the artists from the professional art ensemble of Harbin present.

The second program was contemporary Latin dance presented by Ma Lin, Zhao Wei, Guo Xiaohua and Zhang Ling.

Their performance was characterized by amorous postures, crazy romance, robustness and powerfulness with both masculine strength and feminine beauty. It broadened the view of the audience and was spoken highly of by people. The head of the song and dance troupe of the city made a decision on the site, "Are you willing to work in our troupe after graduation? Your dance and singing level has met with the international standards."

The third program was one act from Othello, a famous Italian tenor opera. Othello went on an expedition to beat the invading enemy and returned with victory. His tenor was accompanied by his inner joy. He was longing to see his beautiful wife whom he hadn't seen for a long time. However, with the instigation of the enemy, he doubted his beloved had an affair with other, "had an adultery with another man and wasn't loyal to him", etc. Therefore, he stamped with fury. He was a short-tempered army man himself.

He got rude and aggressive. Before taking revenge on his love by murdering, he expressed his inner trouble through his painful singing. The act was quite heart-shaking. A standing ovation was won. During the performance, his emotions, hatred and love were vividly delivered, which made people sympathize with him. Paradoxical inner world of Othello was expressed through the artistic technique of opera. To kill or to love, that's a question. It showed his attachment to his love and meanwhile demonstrated his hatred for her unfaithfulness to love. All this made Othello not know what to do. Yingge acted Othello out vividly on the stage.

The stage of Heilongjiang University was the stage where men of talents came out in succession. During the show, Yingge achieved great success. Classmates present applauded him for a long while. He took a bow for several times because the audience strongly requested him to have another performance. Yingge was simply the contemporary Dai Yuqiang.

8. Rack His Brains for New Locomotive Design of Graduation

After transferring to regular college courses from preparatory courses, Yingge set up a greater goal for himself. In the four years of study, he was bent on succeeding his profession, accomplishing something and making some breakthroughs so as to be fully prepared for going to work in future. As a contemporary undergraduate, he should possess a pioneering, ambitious and inspiring spirit. He shouldn't just follow the routines like having meals, going to class and leaving class, and shouldn't focus on what's explained in the textbook only. In addition to digesting what the teachers taught in class, more importantly, he needed to apply basic theories into practice and return to his work to innovate, transform science and technology into productivity, which was the ultimate goal of his.

Minds always guided actions. With a clear goal in sight, Yingge listened to the teacher carefully in class and went to the library after class to look up new knowledge related with what's told by the teacher in class. He paid special attention to the frontier technologies both home and abroad, and check whether there were new discoveries and new supplement or not.

Yingge went to the library to refer to relevant materials after class every day, which was an important step of his daily life. On Saturdays, his classmates invited him to the dance ball but he refused because he tried to cherish his precious time. Yingge went to the library in the afternoon and stayed there until 10:00pm when the library was closed. He wouldn't leave until the teacher on shift came to remind him, "It's time to close the library. Go back and sleep!". Sometimes the teacher would tell him for several times.

Every time Yingge would select a dozen of books from the shelves including both Chinese and Russian works and started reading them on his desk while taking notes carefully.

According to what he learned in class, railway transportation locomotives in contemporary world included steam locomotives, diesel locomotives and electric locomotives in the world. The most advanced was electronic suspension train which was still under experiment. The second generation of high-speed electric locomotives was being experimented in domestic locomotive factories. Steam locomotives were being gradually weeded out due to severe fire coal pollution and small power. At present, China was trying out the second generation of diesel locomotives to replace steam locomotives.

Yingge couldn't help thinking after class: Why can't we create the most advanced third generation of electric locomotives of the world which had no pollution to the air with the rapidest speed of 250 to 400km/h, low transportation cost, fewer operators and higher efficiency. After reading varied materials, Yingge found that electric locomotives had much superiority which had been used for transportation by quite a few advanced countries in the world such as Germany, France, America, Russia and Japan. Besides, it had a great carrying capacity which was three to four times greater than that of ordinary locomotives, and its speed was one to three times greater.

Yingge had made up his mind since then to design and create a kind of new electric locomotive so as to contribute to the high speed and heavy haulage goals of China's railways. Thinking of this, he was so excited that he wanted to start it right now.

Yingge posed lots of questions in class which even got the teachers and made them feel embarrassed. Later on, Yingge changed that and went to the teachers' office to ask questions.

Yingge was studious with a spirit of exploration so he had acquired plenty of knowledge. He had new understanding of the structure and design of electric locomotives. What's taught in class and written in the textbooks were not able to satisfy his demand anymore. He went to Northern Locomotive Research Institute which just started studies on electric locomotives for surveys in summer and winter holidays, consulted with experts, studied design solutions, and proposed his own opinions: solid theoretical foundation should be combined with practices; the design should aim at the world's advanced standard while meeting with national conditions.

Yingge learned through surveys and consultation with domestic and foreign studies that there's no unique high-speed electric locomotive with the latest streamline in the world so far. Yingge with the spirit of a path-breaker and his knowledge brought about a brave idea of designing a rocket-like electric locomotive which would have small air friction during operation with greater speed. Modern locomotive head was flat so the resistance was too much, which wasted energy and affected the speed.

Yingge was determined to study a new locomotive head which would be a extremely beautiful and grand streamline rocket head. Therefore, Yingge collected plenty of materials from hydromechanics study to mechanics of materials, theoretical mechanics to quantum mechanics. He studied the argumentation plans one by one. Besides, he studied the range of the spotlight at the front of the driver's compartment. Urgent braking was a crucial structure. The current range of 800 meters would be increased to 2,500 meters while the locomotive horsepower was increased to 8,000 from 3,000, thus realizing heavy load, greater amount and faster speed. In terms of braking, the steam braking would be transformed to hydraulic pressure with double electromagnetism braking. The train could be stopped anytime with high-speed braking.

Through over two years' exquisite design, Yingge worked out the rough draft. He went to the factories to ask for the opinions of technicians and experts about his draft. After that, he revised and re-designed. By doing so, he's also preparing for the topic of his graduation paper defense.

After repeated inspection and revisions, Yingge finalized his draft and came up with an excellent and top design which was not only the latest in the country but also stood out in the world. The design was praised by a foreign professor working in the research institute. He thought it's characteristic, innovative and the most advanced streamline rocket head in the world.

With changes of the seasons and as time elapsed, Yingge had completed his four years' study in Heilongjiang University. Because of his great efforts and the combination of theories with practice, his academic performance in both theory and practice was far better than his classmates. In addition to learning theories in class, he spent all his time in drawing, designing, looking up materials and proving his design solutions in factories every day. His classmates looked at him with new eyes.

Chief Engineer Liu was an electric locomotive expert who once studied in Germany. He helped and instructed Yingge a lot. Professor Ma of Heilongjiang University had provided great instructions about the theoretical calculation of the major spare parts of the locomotive, locomotive structure and other topics.

Such innovative electric locomotive—rocket head was regarded as unique in structure, advanced and feasible by experts and personnel of the same profession who thought it could be finalized. Next, a model needed to be worked out according to the drawing. Yingge worked hard day and night and made the model in person. Everything came to those who waited. With the help of the workers and engineers in the past one-odd month, the rocket head electric locomotive model was completed and colored with red, white and blue. It appeared especially grand, luxury, novel and bright. It's named "Innovation No. 1".

Yingge frequented the factory to make models. Due to overloaded work and study, Yingge often coughed in class. His classmates and teachers asked him to go for checkup in the hospital. The result showed that Yingge's tuberculosis was aggravated so he needed to be hospitalized. It's only two months before he graduated. He thought: how can I abandon my love "Innovation No. 1" at such critical moment? Yingge wouldn't stay in the hospital no matter how. However, his disease didn't allow that. The doctor said, "Your life will be endangered if you insist so." With the order of the leader, Yingge had to give in. In the hospital, he kept revising his graduation paper while being cured.

Yingge thought to himself: I will participate in the graduation paper defense. It seemed that he didn't know what "death" was because of his indomitable perseverance. In his opinion, learning was more important even than his life. He would keep studying until he died. Some people said he's that kind of person who's not afraid of going to "crematory".

He stayed in the hospital for two months and he's getting better. The paper defense day was coming. Yingge requested the doctor to approve his advanced discharge from the hospital so that he could go take part in the defense. The doctor just couldn't understand why he would rather go study than stay in the hospital for treatment. He wondered whether Yingge feared death or not because he seemed the opposite.

Yingge told the doctor, "Dear doctor, you don't know how many difficulties I have experienced. I know I am lucky and I won't die. In the past when I worked in Harbin, I had many times of narrow escapes. The crematory doesn't welcome me. Just don't worry! People can only live once. I can only have one graduation paper defense in my lifetime. It's an important moment. I just won't miss it for the world."

Yingge had spent five years in Heilongjiang University. He even studied in the coldest time of winter and the hottest time of summer. He had fought hard along the way. He worked day and night. Now it's the last station. How could he stop?

The doctor was moved by his sincerity and persistence. It seemed that his mind already drifted to the defense classroom. If the doctor kept holding him, his disease might get worse. He'd better let Yingge go to the university! The doctor gave Yingge plenty of medicines prescribed for ten days and exhorted him repeatedly, "You must take medicine and have injection in the infirmary on time. Don't give up the treatment." Yingge bowed profoundly to the medical staff and indicated that he would do what they told him. The doctors and nurses in the hospital came to see off this persistent and strong young man.

Yingge finally left the hospital. After going back to school, he was again buried in the topic which he had longed for so much. There were two days left before the graduation paper defense date. The topic had been announced.

The topic: Study on Contemporary Streamline Rocket Head Electric Locomotives

Respondent: Yingge, Class 1, Grade 5, Locomotive Department

Defense date: August 28

Venue: The academic lecture room

Participants: Dr. Zhang Zhen, professor and doctor of Heilongjiang University who once studied in Moscow Jiaotong University, Academician Zhang Chunsheng, professor of dynamics from Harbin Institute of Technology.

Evanoff, professor and doctor of Graduate School, Heilongjiang University, and Leningrad Engineering Institute

Mattrove, doctoral supervisor of Heilongjiang University and professor of Moscow State University

Otte Rovsky, professor of Beijing Jiaotong University

Besides, over ten people such as doctors, postgraduates, professors, candidate doctors, principal and academician dean of Graduate School, Heilongjiang University, would be present in the defense.

The defense topic was novel with higher aim, broadened thinking and extensive knowledge so it attracted lots of undergraduates. The room was packed.

The defense began. Although Yingge's heartbeat got faster, he's confident because of his daily efforts. Being composed and having an ace up his sleeve, he went to the rostrum with his locomotive model in his arms, and turned on the projector. He bowed keenly to all teachers and undergraduates present. He started in Russian, "I would like to extend my sincere thanks to you for sparing time to participate in my graduation paper defense. I would be happy to hear your opinions."

Yingge introduced in Russian his design thought, main structure features and the latest study achievements in electric locomotives in the world today. Detailed argument was made from the internal design to the external shape of the locomotive, from the application of high technology to industrialized manufacture. It's a feasible plan which adapted foreign things for Chinese use based on current industries of China, transformed China's current locomotives to integration and made them meet with international standards. It's been Yingge's guiding ideology to have China's electric locomotive design innovation listed among the international top ones since the very beginning when he started designing the rocket head electric locomotive.

Doctor Zhang Zhen of Heilongjiang University, "Speaking of adapting foreign things for Chinese use, what new international technologies have you referred to in your design?"

Yingge, "Today, with rapid development of science and technology, high-techs have emerged in endlessly in many countries of the world which compete with each other. Therefore, we can't keep our door closed. Instead, we should go global and introduce their technologies. Only in this way can we enhance our technology sooner and contribute to the accelerated development of China's socialist construction. According to the materials I have read, at present the following countries have made great achievements in electric locomotives: Germany, France and Britain in European, Japan in Asia, America and Canada in North America. These countries possess something in electric locomotives which we can draw upon."

"The common thing between the electric locomotive designs of Germany and France is that their pointed head has small resistance. The locomotive head in Britain is trapezoid while it's round in Japan and fish head in Russia. While others' strong points can be seen in my design, it has its uniqueness, that is, the design of streamline rocket head. Such structure and shape bring about very small resistance. In particular, when it's running rapidly, it has smaller air friction compared with other simulated models. In hydrodynamics test, its resistance is two to three times smaller. Its speed is accelerated. Meanwhile, it can save energy and reduce emission. Therefore, the design is superior than similar foreign products."

The doctoral supervisor Mattrove asked, "Compared with international locomotive engines in the world, what is the superiority of the engine in your design? Is it home-made or imported?"

Yingge answered, "The locomotive engine in my design is home made. It can save foreign exchange and reduce cost. More importantly, we should follow the domestication path based on our industrial level. We can produce large advanced electric locomotives even without import, which can better demonstrate our country's founding policy of 'independence and self-reliance'. Moreover, we have Dalian Locomotive Factory, Sifang Locomotive Factory, Beijing Locomotive Factory and Zhuzhou Locomotive Factory, etc. We still have lots of large electric locomotive factories and we are capable of producing large power traction electric locomotives to satisfy the demand for such locomotives. That's my guiding ideology." Yingge's answer really convinced Professor Mattrove.

Professor Mattrove said, "You value scientific outlook on development and the spirit of independent innovation, which is worth learning." He nodded and praised that China's undergraduates were awesome and their fate was related with that of the country.

Dr. Osterrove, professor of Southwest Jiaotong University, asked, "The speed of your electric locomotive is up to 350 to 400km/h. With such rapid speed, have you ever considered the friction and too much heat problem of the spare parts? How do you deal with that?"

Yingge seemed assured, "Thank you, professor. The problem you mentioned is very important. The high-speed operation of the locomotive is bound to strengthen the attrition rate of spare parts. Besides, they need to bear the high temperature and too much heat during adjustment. To solve the problem, we need a good lubrication system first and second we need to have good alloy materials. China's Dalian Diesel Locomotive Factory has solved it with its strong technical strength. Their application of closed automatic refueling lubrication system has effectively reduced the friction among spare parts. For some key spare parts, contemporary plasma and supersonic speed surface spray ceramics alloy technique is adopted. It's wear-resisting and can resist high temperature of as high as 350°C. Therefore, we can be totally relieved since Dalian Diesel Locomotive Factory produces the key spare parts for us."

At this time, Dr. Zhang Tiansheng, chief engineer of Dalian Diesel Locomotive Factory who once studied in America, stood up, "Yingge visited our factory during holidays. He did the experiment in our 400km/h locomotive laboratory with our technology. After one day's high-speed operation, the spray ceramics alloy bearings he designed passed the test. Hence, we are confident in processing qualified spare parts for Yingge's new locomotive." The speech of the chief engineer fully approved and supported Yingge's design.

Russian Professor Molotov of Beijing Jiaotong University asked, "If roadblock showed up ahead during high-speed operation and urgent braking is required, can your braking device do that?"

Yingge answered, "During high-speed operation, the locomotive has great inertia. According to Newton's second law, $F=ma$. Only when the braking force $F \geq ma$ can the locomotive stop rapidly. The brake of ordinary locomotives is pneumatic braking which has small force and slow effects. It's not suitable for huge power and high-speed electric locomotives. Two ways of hydraulic brake and electromagnetic brake are adopted in my design. The simultaneous application of the two methods can work along. F braking is greater than ma. The experiment shows that such braking force is five to seven times greater than ordinary pneumatic braking. Besides, the operation is simple; the braking is quick; the start-up, operation and stoppage are convenient. Besides, it will run stably without accidents."

Dr. Zhang, professor of Harbin Institute of Technology who once studied in France, "Usually when a locomotive runs with heavy load or overload, it can only carry 2,000t to 2,500t. The load for your locomotive is 8,000t. How does the locomotive overcome such great inertia when it starts up? What kind of measures will you take to realize stable start-up?"

Yingge said, "Ingenuity is more important than physical work for anything. I have thought about it in the design process. Heavy-load trains can't be dragged by force. The electromotor will be burned and the connection hooks will be broken if operation rules are not followed. While designing, I let the hard spring to support the compartments and especially the head connector. When the train starts, it should go backward to press the gaps between hooks tight. After that, the head should be started first because the force will be small. After repeated dragging, the compartments won't burn the engine during the operation. There's another more reliable method, that is, the start-up engine is installed in each compartment. In this way, it will be a lot easier to start. The strength of multiple engines is great. It can be adopted."

Professor Zhang got excited, "You drove trains before, didn't you? You seemed an insider! It's not easy to answer this question. Those who don't have experience in driving trains won't be able to answer it. Quite good! Very professional! Very professional! You were very excellent train driver, I guess. You are so experienced!"

Yingge was touched, "Thank you for your encouragement, professor!"

Chief Engineer Zhang from Dalian Locomotive Factory who once studied in France asked again, "When the electric locomotive is running at a high speed, the parking signal range should cover a greater scope. In particular, at night, if the range is small and the train can't stop in time, it's likely to cause collision. What do you think of this?"

Yingge said with self-assurance, "The station signal is an important device for electric locomotives to start and stop. The spotlight range of ordinary locomotive head is 500m and it's only be used for slow trains with a speed of 70 to 400km/h. The speed of electric locomotives is 250 to 400km/h so the spotlight range should be over 2,000m. I design my locomotive according to this range. High-tech optics principles are adopted and the radiotelescope theories of Russia are referred to. With electronic spotlight, the range can be up to 1,800 to 2,200m. It has reached technical standards through repeated tests at the stations. Even if it's cloudy or foggy, the range can be 1,500m. In case of bad weather, the driver only needs to press the long spotlight range."

"Do you have the test report?" Yingge answered in high spirit, "Yes!" Yingge took out the test report of the stations. The chief engineer was very happy and said affirmatively, "The data is complete and precise with advanced methods. It's an innovative technology."

The chief engineer from Tsitsihar Vehicle Factory who once studied in Germany said, "In the defense we can see Yingge's paper is outstanding. I think his paper has met the standards for a master's degree thesis." The chief engineer faced towards Yingge sincerely and amiably, "I am wondering whether you can transfer this or not. On behalf of the factory, I accept your technology and drawing. You are welcome to come to work in the technology office of my factory as my assistant after your graduation." Yingge's young heart was stirred after receiving such appreciation.

Professor Wang of Jiaotong University also gave his offer.

Professor Zhang Zhen, supervisor of Yingge and the host of the defense, said, "Do you have any problem and opinion about Yingge's defense. If not, please grade it."

They unanimously showed the sign of Excellent Paper, Five marks.

Yingge expressed his thanks in Russian, "First, I would like to extend my thanks to teachers and experts for giving me instructions in the process of writing this paper. With your help, I tried my best to apply theories to practices, transform science and technology to productivity. 'Consult with workers and experts more', I have borne Professor Zhang's words in mind. I wouldn't have written such an excellent paper but for the effective instructions of my supervisor."

As he was saying, he bowed affectionately to his supervisor Professor Zhang Zhen, and also bowed respectfully and profoundly to judges present.

Yingge continued, "I need to consult with the principal of Heilongjiang University about the matter of technical transfer. However, there's one thing I want to solemnly announce: I won't take the technical transfer fees which will all be donated to the university as scientific research funds so as to reward those classmates and teachers who achieve something and make them stride forward bravely on the road of scientific research and win glories for our university."

The principal of Heilongjiang University hugged Yingge cordially and said, "I am much enlightened by Yingge's graduation paper defense. Yingge has set an example for our future defense. In future, when we evaluate the graduation paper of a bachelor's degree, master's degree or a doctoral degree, we need to see whether it's helpful to production or not, whether it can be transformed into productivity to solve production and actual scientific research problems or not and whether it's innovative or not. After reviewing Yingge's paper, some factory leaders want technical transfer on site. I think it's good and it demonstrates the value of his paper. Tsitsihar Locomotive Factory has good taste. It wants to introduce both technologies and personnel. Practices show that excellent products are out of the question if excellent personnel are missing."

In the end, the principal of Heilongjiang University said with emotions, "On behalf of the defense committee, I would like to award 'bachelor's degree' to Yingge but his excellent paper is qualified for a master's degree. Therefore, I will award him 'master's degree' as well."

Dr. Feng, the academic dean, on behalf of the graduation allocation committee, said, "If Yingge agrees, we hope that you can stay to study for the doctoral degree."

The speech of the principal won warm applause amid which Yingge's excellent graduation paper defense wrapped up.

While leaving the defense room, Yingge's heart was going to pop out. He's so excited. In an instant, he thought, "My efforts, my suffering and my striving finally paid off well. No pains, no gains. In future, I will guard against arrogance and follow the 'footprint' to keep striving forward! The world is my oyster."

9. Risk His Life to Fight Floods and Provide Relief

The five-year study in Heilongjiang University was finally ended. After graduation, classmates parted with each other and most of them left their alma mater, leaving Yingge and few classmates stay in the university temporarily. They were the elites of all students.

In that summer, Harbin was stricken by the storm disaster. The water level of Songhua River kept rising and the flood exceeded the warning line. Harbin city asked for emergency help! Again and again! All citizens of the city must be mobilized immediately to fight against the flood because once the Songhua River was breached, the city would be a world of waters and inestimably great losses would be caused to the people and national economy.

The flood was ruthlessly swallowing thousands of rural households and their crops which they lived on. The upstream of the Songhua River was breached and the entire rural area looked like a vast sea. Crops were inundated in the flood. Both the urban and rural areas of the city needed help! The provincial and municipal governments called on people to take emergency actions to fight against the flood and provide relief as well as sparing no effort to guard Harbin!

Yingge was burning with anxiety. He immediately organized several League members to go to the university leaders and apply for going to the frontline of the flood resistance. They wanted to guard their alma mater, people and Harbin with their lives!

Yingge was allocated to the lifeboat as he wished to save those people struggling in the flooded households. The little boat ushered in the village where everywhere was water. Yingge got off the boat to look for people who weren't transferred one household by another. The little hill opposite was packed with villagers. At this time, the cries of children were heard and Yingge searched by following the sound.

Yingge entered a small rural courtyard where the water was over three feet deep. Three bungalows were soaked in the water and the water already reached the bed edge.

Yingge entered the house and was taken aback. A woman and a five-year-old boy were crying desperately and in panic in the house. The scene shocked Yingge who immediately went up to hold the woman's hand and carried the children in his arms. After crossing the courtyard, they went towards the little boat. However, the little boat was already full. Yingge was so anxious that he didn't know what to do. At such critical moment, he put aside his own safety and only wanted to save the mother and son. Suddenly he saw a tree nearby. He put the boy on the branch and fastened him with his belt. Then he bent over and let the middle-aged woman climb onto the tree by stepping on him. Yingge thought he must save them. He took off his pants, dried them and fastened her onto the tree. He let her hang in there and said, "We are coming back soon." He walked away from the tree in a hurry.

The woman cried, "Good brother. You risked your life to save us. How can we return such great favor!"

Yingge said, "Sister, you two take care of yourself. Goodbye!" He's searching another tree for rescue in the water.

A big door happened to drift here from the upstream. Yingge seized the door and floated downstream. Yingge had no strength to control his direction and just randomly drifted with the door. After a while, Yingge saw a glimpse of hope again, a little boat was coming towards him ahead and he was dragged to the boat. He was so cold that he couldn't speak. The people on the boat gave him a piece of clothes and hot water. He finally recovered.

Yingge said, "Oh, god. A mother and his son in Chenjiatun were still on the tree. If we don't go save them, the flood will drown the tree and they will die. Please go save them."

However, it's a vast of sea. Where could they find Chenjiatun? They were in a pickle. Under the guidance of Yingge, the boat went against the water. After a long while, a green tree finally came into sight. The little boat sped up to find that the mother and son were there. The water had covered the woman's legs and she's holding her son tightly. Seeing her savior really come back, the woman cried. Since they were saved, Yingge was finally relaxed.

Then the woman cried, kneed down and kowtowed towards her savior for several times. Later, the boat went back to the opposite bank. At this time, it's getting dark.

Yingge returned to the university, exhausted. He rested for several days. The flood hadn't retreated yet. The ferocious flood was going to breach the dam. Once the dam broke down.... Oh, God! The university was in danger again. Yingge ran to the flood resistance office of the university and asked for tasks. In the end, the leader approved that Yingge went to repair the dam at the frontline of flood resistance, which was the most difficult and bitter task. He carried sandbags of about 100 jin on his shoulder and walked for over one li. Yingge did that for three days. The leader asked him to rest but he just refused. The wind and waves surged recently. If the dam wasn't fixed in time, there's a danger of breaching.

Yingge didn't flinch in case of emergency. Many dams and important sections were in danger of breaching and were guarded by special personnel. The dam taken charge of by Yingge was the most dangerous one. However, it didn't ask for emergency help. The leaders in the command department wondered why they didn't see Yingge and sent a team to the section for inspection. After the inspection team arrived, they were shocked. People were holding hands together hard and formed a wall of human bodies. They resisted against the flood with their own bodies and protected the dam which was going to be breached. Yingge and comrades protected the dam, national property and life safety of people with their lives. Their behaviors moved God, moved the leaders and all other people. Later on, a more intense and brave trend of flood-fighting and emergency rescues was staged.

People's strength was invincible. At the celebration meeting after victory over the flood, ten young people including Yingge were awarded the title of Flood Resistance Hero. Wearing red flowers, they waved their hands to extend their thanks to those people present. Yingge's enthusiastic life was again realized. Hence, Yingge had left the brave "footprint" during the process of flood-fighting and emergency rescues.

10. Where Is the Way after Graduation

Yingge had achieved excellent performance in both Russian exam and engineering design during the graduation exam of Heilongjiang University. The leaders of the university and Yingge's supervisor were quite satisfied and happy. When leaving his alma mater--Heilongjiang University, Yingge's supervisor Professor Anna was reluctant to part with such an excellent student and hugged him with tears full in her eyes.

The Student Office of Heilongjiang University sent Yingge to work in Bureau of Foreign Experts Affairs of Ministry of Foreign Affairs in Beijing according to his excellent performance in multiple aspects. Here he could go abroad on a regular basis and conduct academic exchanges in the world's advanced countries. It's the ideal institution longed for and desired by all graduates. However, it's a pity that Yingge couldn't go to Beijing and couldn't work in such a good institution as Ministry of Foreign Affairs, which was unexpected for others. He himself felt depressed as well.

The instructor sent for Yingge and asked him with curiosity, "Why on earth can't you go to Beijing. I just can't understand you."

Yingge said with tears in eyes, "I am much obliged for the university and teachers' deep affection for me."

Yingge continued, "My parents are getting old and weak. They live in Dalian and nobody take care of them. I can't leave them alone!"

Yingge's face was covered with tears, "In order to repay my parents who have brought me up and perform my filial duty, I have to give up the work in Beijing, the superior life there and the glamorous capital."

Yingge said, "I want to be sent to Dalian. Although it's a bit difficult in Dalian and my house is only ten square meters, I still want to work in Jiaotong University as a teacher who can train personnel for our motherland. Besides, I can stay near my parents." He continued, "According to traditional Chinese philosophy, of all virtues filial piety is the most important. I should perform my duties so that when they leave this world, I won't regret."

After graduation from Heilongjiang University, many institutions vied for hiring him because of his outstanding performance in the graduation paper defense. Jiaotong University employed Yingge as it wished.

Part IV Enthusiastic Life

1. Step onto the University Rostrum

Yingge came to the coastal city Dalian with beautiful scenery from the northern ice city Harbin, which was a great turning of Yingge's life.

Facing the waves on the sea, Yingge's heart surged like those insurgent waves. When looking back, Yingge couldn't help thinking the past had been an eventful times: childhood with difficulties; trials, danger and fighting in the virgin forest; colorfulness in college life; assiduous pursuit of academic peak. He had gone through hardships in his youth. He had explored and paid out. His youth had been shining all the time. Yingge thought: poor parents raised me up and my motherland which was not wealthy trained me. The love of my parents and motherland would be engraved on my mind forever. It's time to repay motherland and parents.

During the days when the sky was high and clouds were pale, and the harvest was around the corner, Yingge came to Jiaotong University for sign-up with his longing, hope and determination, and wanted to contribute his youth and strength to the education cause of his motherland.

Jiaotong University was a well-known university of Ministry of Railways. Students who passed the national entrance exam and were admitted to the university would feel extremely proud and glorious. The lawn was verdant adorned with colorful and beautiful flowers. There were all kinds of solemn and good-looking building facilities such as teaching buildings, laboratories, school-run factory, research institute, library and student apartments. The academic atmosphere was strong and the environment was beautiful. It's a vast ocean of youth during class break.

At the teachers' symposium, Principal Dai introduced, "Our university must absorb plenty of new personnel to join us in order to become the country's first-rate university. All of you come from national key universities and are excellent personnel and elites. You will become the backbone of our university so you must give full scope to your strengths. Comrade Yingge is the excellent graduate from Heilongjiang University and his graduate paper has won Excellent Master's Degree Thesis title. It's pretty awesome!"

Principal Dai continued, "Besides, students such as Ma Jun from Shanghai Jiaotong University, Liu Tao from North Jiaotong University, Zhang Ke from Southwest Jiaotong University and Wu Yun from Peking University have passed the thesis defense for master's degree and doctoral degree. Our university has hired so many excellent personnel which are a great wealth and treasure of ours. Here, on behalf of Jiaotong University, I would like to extend warm welcome to top students who come to sign up, and wish you make abundant achievements in teaching and scientific research as well as training a batch of innovative personnel and science masters."

Principal Dai asked Yingge to make a speech as the representative of the new teachers.

Yingge was full of pride and stood up, "We all come from national key universities which have trained us for five years. It's time to repay the Party and our motherland in Jiaotong University. We will never fail the principal and we will devote our lifetime efforts to the education cause of Jiaotong University. Just as what we did when we were students, we will work hard, live an enthusiastic life, work indomitably, influence students with our actions, set up an example for our students, be a model for them, train the students of Jiaotong University into science elites who will work with perseverance, be brave to strive and good at climbing and undergraduates who will reassure the Party and people. Our graduates are not only approved in the country but also appreciated by well-known universities of the world after they go to work in society. They are outstanding even among foreign students." He spoke louder and said excitedly, "The function of individual wealth to social progress is small and temporary. The training of personnel is great and permanent to social development. I would like to be completely dedicated to our motherland's education cause and live up to the expectations of the Party and people." Yingge's speech greatly encouraged young teachers present.

Yingge fully realized that he should influence students with true love, education them with true words and teach them with true knowledge. He should love all students with fairness. Only when teachers influenced students with true feelings and students understood teachers' feelings can students listen to the teachers' edification, like teachers and be closer to teachers. Only when teachers told the truth to students can they trust and admire teachers. No matter what you said, how could you teach students if you didn't have true knowledge? You were harming the younger generation, weren't you? It's sinful to train useless personnel for your motherland.

Based on the spirit mentioned above, Yingge conduct surveys on students at the beginning of the semester to learn about their learning conditions and what kind of teachers they liked, what kind of lecture were welcome in class and what contents they would be interested, etc. Yingge obtained data from the students and applied theories to students in order to impart knowledge and educate people. His education goal was to train students into people with both talents and morals, independent innovation, ways of thinking, combination of theories and practices as well as endurance of hardships. He deeply knew that he must have more water if he wanted to give students a glass of water. His current capability was far insufficient so he needed to work harder. According to Yingge, the fact that some students didn't listen to the teacher carefully in class and couldn't concentrate was caused by the teacher's insufficient teaching level. The source didn't lie in students but teachers. They failed to lecture knowledge feasibly so students' enthusiasm couldn't be motivated. It all came down to the reason that teachers' strategy was bad and foundation was not solid. How could they blame students?

The academic dean assigned heavy teaching tasks to Yingge who had to teach both the basic courses for graduates and major courses for undergraduates, which was a huge challenge for a new teacher. Usually, it took five years to grow from an assistant teacher intern and assistant teacher to a lecture. With his solid foundation, assiduous work in research, vivid and conscientious lecture, high lecture quality and good effects, Yingge was well reviewed among students. He was promoted to a lecture in two years only.

Yingge's quick promotion was inseparable from his work performance. Most of his students were outstanding and some were elites. All he thought was that the country was in badly need of excellent personnel. Greater efforts must be made to let students innovate and invent from the perspective of scientific outlook on development, tackle key science and technology problems of the world, do great things with a pioneering spirit, possess the dominance of "if I can't do it, who can?" and the "ambition" of being brave to occupy the highland of technologies.

In order to train students, Yingge not only prepared lessons well and taught what's told in the textbooks but also led students to the factories for scientific research. In this way, they located topics during production and transformed scientific research achievements into productivity. He still remained the same with his student time. He studied hard to solve key problems and practiced on site. He often went to conduct surveys and fought indomitably in order to train innovative undergraduates.

2. True Love Demonstrated at a Blizzard Night

Yingge was writing something in his little room of his home while kept murmuring the foreign language. His table was stacked with books, charts and models. Wall maps hang all over the room. It's very cold in the room. Sometimes he rubbed his hands and sometimes he stamped his feet. It's only about 10°C in the room and it's snowing outside. His old mother was patching clothes for him and urged him, "It's time to go to the university. You need to make up missed lessons for students."

His mother went out to the courtyard to find that the snow was really heavy and it's already over one foot thick. She went inside the house and said, "Kid, it's heavy snow outside and it's thick. Can you still go lecture for students? The road is not smooth. Hopefully there will be no accident! The snow is really worrying!" His mother kept nagging.

Yingge was preparing the lesson heart and soul, and didn't notice the snow outside. He went out to check. Indeed the snow was heavy. The northwest wind was howling and blowing hard.

The road was closed due to the snow so there's no bus. He had to ride his bicycle. His mother persuaded, "It's not easy to ride a bicycle with such thick snow. Stay at home today, my love. The leaders and students will understand you. You can go tomorrow."

Yingge said, "No, mum. I have to go to class. How can I educate my students to overcome difficulties in future if I just don't go due to the snow and flinch in front of difficulties! Students are waiting for me in the classroom. It's not one or two. They are many. I can't let them down! Their study time is very precious and the homework is tight. They spare their extracurricular time in learning German from me."

His old mother said, "You are just making up lessons for them. It's off hours, not regular courses. The university doesn't pay you for that and neither do those students. It's completely out of your loving heart. You want to help them with their exam for graduate exam...... Who will help you if anything happens to you on the road? I will be worried about you! My son, I am really worried about your going outside in a snowy day."

"Mum, please forgive me. I have to go to lecture for students." Yingge's mother said, "I can't do anything if you really want to go. At least have a bowl of hot porridge and warm up before you leave. It's cold outside! What should I do if you catch cold and fell sick?"

Yingge agreed, "Well, get me a bowl of hot porridge." The old mother went to the kitchen and poked the furnace with the hook. After the porridge was heated, she put it in a bowl and gave it and pickles to Yingge. With fondness, the mother watched Yingge finished it.

Yingge carried his bag and rode his bicycle to the university. The snow was heavy and it's headwind, Yingge had to shove the bicycle along. After a while, he suddenly saw a pregnant woman sitting beside the road. She's groaning painfully with her hands on his belly. At this time, there were few people on the road.

Yingge went up and asked, "What's wrong, sister?" "I am going to give birth. Just now I fell down. Oh, god, I can't take it anymore." The snow was so heavy and it's so cold. What to do? The pregnant seemed anguish and sat there helplessly. She watched Yingge desperately.

Yingge said, "Don't worry. Don't worry. Hold on. I will help you onto my bicycle and send you to the hospital. Sit on the back seat." Yingge thought: Two people's lives were in his hand in such a bitter cold winter day with heavy snow and billowing north wind. Yingge looked around and there's no bus on the road. The bus was stopped due to the snow. There's nothing else he could do. He went to the hospital and moved forward with difficulty as the woman sat on his bicycle. After arriving at the hospital, he let the pregnant woman sit down. Then he hurried to register and pay money. He left her to the nurse and helped the nurse send her to the delivery room. He said goodbye to the woman. The nurse asked the woman, "Is he your husband?" The woman answered, "No. We don't know each other. We met each other on the way." The nurse said, "What a good guy! He saved you two. If you are a bit later, your child may have been born in the blizzard. How dangerous it would be!"

Yingge pushed his bicycle and walked towards the university in a nervous state. The farther he went, the more difficult it was. It's hard to push the bicycle due to the headwind. He had to carry the bicycle on his shoulder.

After an assiduous trip, Yingge doddered along and finally arrived at the university. He fell down for several times on the way and snow was all over him. It's dark. The university gate was closed and Yingge shouted to the guard.

The guard asked, "It's so late, teacher Yingge. Is there anything urgent in the university?" "I am here for a lesson." "It's off work. Most of students have left. Who will you teach? It's so cold and the snow is so heavy. How did you get here?" The old guard shook his head and looked at Yingge with confusion. Yingge was a snowman now. "Students are waiting for me in the classroom." The old guard said, "Go upstairs." The old man shook his head with resignation.

Yingge came to the classroom and students stood up with surprise. Snow was all over Yingge. Frozen ice residues could be seen on his face and mustache. He was just like an alien visitor and students were stunned and didn't know what to do and what to say. A student handed a towel to Yingge for wiping out his face, and helped him take off his coat. Students hurriedly clean the ice and snow on their teacher's coat. Some girl students were so moved that they wept with hands covering their faces.

Yingge went up and comforted them, "I'm fine. Don't worry. Don't be sad."

Yingge said, "Well, thank you. I am late for some reason today. Sorry. Please forgive me."

Students went back to their own seats. It's oral German practice today.

Class began. Yingge greeted in German, "Guten Tag! Hi, girls and boys!"

They returned in unison in German, "Good evening, teacher!" Today, their voice was a lot louder than usual.

Yingge said in German, "Good evening! I am going to start. Let's review what we have learned first. Before beginning the lesson, I want to praise you for your hard-working spirit. At a snowy night, you still come to the class on time and waiting for me so patiently. It means you have strong desire for knowledge. With your hardworking and enterprising spirits, you are bound to do a good job in German. I feel proud to have students like you. Thank you!"

Soon afterwards, the monitor stood up and said, "We feel proud too to have such good teacher like you. You love us and train us so sincerely. Regardless of the bitterness, you come to class at such a snowy night. On behalf of all students, I would like to pay respect to you! With cordiality, I would like to say: Teacher Yingge, thank you so much!"

Yingge named another student and asked in German, "Why do you still come since the snow is so heavy and it's so cold?"

The student answered in German, "I don't fear any difficulty because I am studying for our motherland!"

He asked another student, "What do you think of this snowy night?"

The student answered, "True love is witnessed with heavy snow and bitter coldness. What you did for us will be unforgettable to me in my lifetime. The example you set for us is a silent order and teaches us to overcome difficulties. In future, many more difficulties will be encountered at both work and study. We will act like you and overcome difficulties. We are sure to succeed!"

"Dear students, is his answer good?" They answered in unison, "Yes!" Yingge hinted the student to sit down. He asked another student, "What about you? What's your opinion about today's lesson?"

The student said, "In future, as long as I think of this blizzard night and our strong love, I will fear no difficulty. You walk here to lecture for us regardless of the blizzard. Your great dedication spirit is the motivation for us to overcome future difficulties. I want to be somebody so I have to learn German and repay your evangelistic education with excellent performance."

"Dear students, the discussion at the blizzard night not only improves your German speaking but also makes me feel that the blizzard can only freeze our body but not our heart. The loving bond between us is kept on our mind. I would like to extend my thanks to you for your true love for me. I am really touched. Thank you for your precious learning spirit for the sake of our motherland. It's worth it for me to come here today! Such pure and lofty feelings between students and the teacher are hard to buy!" Yingge taught some grammar knowledge and wrote some contrast examples between Chinese and German on the blackboard. Students were more careful than usual.

Somebody in the corridor knocked at the door. The old guard shouted, "Class is over. It's already ten. We are going to close the gate!"

Yingge said, "Okay! We are going to dismiss. Dear classmates, let's call it a day and see you!"

"See you!" Students replied their teacher in unison.

Yingge felt so warm, joyful and happy right now. His tiredness and coldness were all gone. Although the road back home was still difficult, he felt much relaxed.

He pushed his bicycle and was going to leave the university in a hurry. He was worried about his mother. The old guard said, "The snow is too heavy. You'd better stay in the dorm here."

Yingge refused, "Thank you but I wanted to go home. Otherwise my mother will be worried."

On the way back home, Yingge thought of the pregnant woman and wondered whether they were safe or not. Therefore, he went to the hospital and asked the doctor who told him the lady gave birth to a little fat baby boy. Both of them went well.

Yingge smiled, "Good, good! Thank you for your help."

Yingge asked the doctor to send his regards to them and he couldn't see them because he had something urgent to do.

After leaving the hospital, he hurried back home and found an old grandpa squatting around the corner of a house. Yingge went up to inquire and learned that he came to the city to look for his son. However, there's no bus due to the snow and he got lost. He's so frozen that he couldn't walk anymore.

It's so cold. If the old man stayed there for a longer time, he would be frozen to death. Yingge couldn't just leave him there. He lifted the old grandpa up and asked him about the address of his son. After looking at the address, he helped the grandpa onto the bicycle and went to look for his son. They passed a little bridge on No. 24, Happy Street, and then turned eastwards. There's no road lamp. His son lived in the first floor. After that, he said goodbye to them and even didn't go inside to have a drink. He continued on his way back home but when he reached home, he didn't see his mother. Yingge was wet with cold sweats. He shouted loud and then went to his neighbors.

An aunt told him, "Your mother was in hospital. She was waiting for you to come back out on the street. She's worried about you so she waited there for a long time. Then she fainted and fell onto the ground. We found her and sent her to the hospital. Just go see her!" After hearing that, Yingge rushed to the hospital. He shouted "Mum" while running! After arriving at the ward, the doctor explained that his mother was too old to stand such bitter coldness. Her blood pressure got high and then fainted. Now she's out of danger after urgent rescue but still had a fever.

Yingge kneed down in front of his mother's bed and cried, "Mother, sorry. I am late. I didn't care you enough, mother! Don't leave me. Otherwise I will miss you so much! I can't live without you, mother! You are my beloved! I didn't create better living conditions for you! How incompetent I am!" The doctor came and pulled him up. He asked Yingge to take care of his mother who's having a fever. Her heart didn't function well either.

Yingge told the hardships his mother had experienced. He cried and narrated, "Doctor, please cure my mother. I can't live without her!"

Yingge turned back to hold his mother's hand tightly as he was speaking. At this time, his mother opened her eyes and finally woke up. They hugged each other and cried. "Oh, my son. I finally see you. My good son! You are back!" "Mother, I am not a good son and I let you stand there waiting for me in the frozen air. I went home late. Sorry mother. Thank God, you can talk to me now! I won't leave you anymore." Mother said, "It's so good that I can see you. I was waiting there and didn't see you come back. I don't know I can get here! Let's go home. I am fine now." The doctor said, "She can't leave now. She should stay here for few more days when her blood pressure is stable."

Yingge thanked the doctor, bowed affectionately to his mother and asked his mother to listen to the doctor, "You stay here and receive the treatment. I will go home first and then come back later."

It's already midnight when he arrived home. He cooked something his mother loved and headed back to the hospital to accompany his mother.

The student whom Yingge taught over three decades ago came to visit Yingge at the beginning of 2012. They hadn't seen each other for many years. Yingge greeted, "How are you, my dear teacher?" Yingge was stunned hearing the amiable address. Lots of changes had happened. The 20-year-old guy in the past now turned into a middle-aged man with grey hair and showed up in front of

Yingge with a capable and experienced appearance. Yingge almost found it hard to recognize him and went up to shake hands with him. Upon a close look, he gradually remembered his young appearance.

The student made a self-introduction, “I am Geng Jian, your student. I am sorry for not visiting you the past years.”

The student recalled, “I will never forget you. At the blizzard night, you pushed your bicycle to go to the university and lecture Germany for us although it’s far from your home. It’s late and you couldn’t go home due to the heavy snow. You sat alone in the classroom to prepare lessons for us. I couldn’t forget your persistence, enthusiasm and selfless spirits. You worked really hard in order to train us into useful personnel and masters. You are a truly good teacher who’s not tired of teaching us!”

Geng Jian continued, “I have made many painstaking and arduous scientific researches. Whenever I come across difficulties at work, I will remember what happened at the blizzard night. Your dedication spirit has been encouraging me all the way and bringing me infinite power.”

“I have passed the national foreign language exam and obtained Level A translation certificate. I went abroad for investigations, symposiums and academic exchanges for several times. On behalf of our country, I cooperated with German Railway Academy of Science to study the most advanced high-speed and heavy-load electric locomotive. I was the chief designer.” Geng Jian narrated.

He went on, “The locomotives our country design so far have met with the world’s advanced standards. I am here to tell you and extend my sincere thanks to you, teacher.”

Yingge felt considerably delighted to learn that his student had made such great achievements and such great contributions to the motherland’s railway cause. His student had become a genuine railway science master. With tears of joy, Yingge and his student hugged each other, “Good! You didn’t let me down!”

The student also talked about other classmates Yingge had taught such as Zhang Xiaoming and Ma Lin who were the high-end talents studying the world's most advanced locomotives.

Yingge said happily, "The teacher only indicates the direction for students but the rest depends on students themselves."

3. Completely Dedicated to Train Top Talents

According to Yingge, education was the foundation underlying all our efforts to build the country and a strong footstone for development of productivity. School was the palace of training innovative personnel. He regarded the rostrum in the classroom as a platform to show his abilities and had dedicated to teaching at the frontline. For him, education was first and foremost important.

To put it simple, Yingge's education philosophy was to impart knowledge and education people among which the latter was the priority. He maintained that the method of educating people was to "persuade sentimentally and rationally". More importantly, sentiment should be the focus. Deep connotations came with profound feelings. Only when teachers treated students as their family could the gap between be narrowed, thus building a harmonious relationship between teachers and students, teachers respected and admired by students and teacher's personality charisma demonstrated.

Chinese ancient civilization advocated, "A strict teacher can train outstanding students. Even if the teacher only teaches you for one day, you have to treat him as your father and show respect!"

In the eyes of Yingge, strict teachers should not be strict with students only. What's more important was that teachers must be demanding for themselves so as to set an example for students. Example was better than precept. They should treat students as their own children. Those teachers who started class and left the class as the ring belled would never train the backbone of the country. Instead, teachers should be completely devoted the great cause of education and put a lot of blood to nurse them in order to achieve something.

Sometimes Yingge thought: There were thousands of undergraduates, postgraduates and doctoral graduates every year. Why did nobody of them ever achieve a Nobel Prize in the past decades? Why did the science and technology fall short of master leaders? Why did no Chinese expert stand on the international science podium and wasn't there the world's extraordinary leader? It's worth the deliberation of college and university experts.

It's wrong, according to Yingge, to have no "swift horses" in colleges, but it's worse to have no potential science masters. The reason was that "talent scout" was missing among teachers! They didn't try to find "swift horses" and didn't instruct the "swift horses" to the right direction.

In Yingge's opinion, as an excellent teacher, a professor, a doctoral supervisor and an educator, teachers shouldn't just see how many theses students had written, how many scientific research projects they had participated and how many books they had published; instead, the key point was to see whether it could be combined with productivity or not. Besides, teachers' education philosophy should be examined. Whether they could instruct students to the road of "masters" and set an example was important. If teachers want to let their students become doctors and masters, they should aim at higher goals.

Just as an excellent coach, he might not be the world champion himself but he could train a world champion. For instance, Sun Haiping, the teacher of Liu Xiang (China Speed), was a case in point. He's an example and a vivid demonstration. Just as the old saying went, "The worthy disciple outdoes his master" and "The later comers surpass the formers."

Yingge was not a diplomatist but he had trained China's science and technology counselor in the embassy in foreign countries and WTO negotiation representatives. Yingge was not a doctor but he trained high-level doctoral graduates.

All in all, teachers shouldn't fear that students would transcend them; instead they should let students stand on their shoulders and climb higher. They should feel glorious and proud for that. It's called selfless contribution.

He told his students to learn how to conduct themselves first before studying knowledge. He said people should have integrity and invincible spirit so as to accomplish something. Those who had an ambition could travel all over the world.

Yingge said, "Only when an excellent teacher possess the hard working spirit of not fearing hardships can he cultivate students who can stand difficulties, hard works, and who will never give up in case of setbacks. Don't think about others' gossip. You need to stick to your belief, carry it through and prove it with facts."

In 1960s, a locomotive factory in Sichuan imported five large automatic machines tools from Germany which were stored in the warehouse. Nobody dared touch it for five years because they couldn't afford it if any damage was caused. Five boxes of German materials and meters were laid idle there and nobody could translate them. One of Yingge's students was allocated to the factory to work with dozens of graduates from national key universities in the workshop. After learning about the situation, Professor Yingge advised him to request the factory to activate those five imported equipment in the warehouse and use them for production. He studied mechanics in Jiaotong University and grasped two foreign languages: Russian and Germany. With Yingge's instructions, he had acquired the pioneering spirit and tenacity. Professor Yingge provided German dictionary for the student. He spent one hard year in the warehouse. He ate, lived and worked in the warehouse, and finally translated the five boxes of German materials into Chinese. With great support of the factory leaders and the instruction of Professor Yingge, the five large equipments were finally put in place and brought about great economic benefits to the factory. Domestic brand products were produced. He was trusted and put in an important position by the factory. Soon he was promoted to the technology department head, workshop manager and later promoted to the chief engineering of the factory. Yingge had two demanding requirements for his students: first, work hard and stand hardships; second, take actions and be brave to innovate.

For Yingge, the more important thing was to emphasize the training of their personality charisma in order to train them into masters. It's an individual's intangible assets, the foundation for his foothold and a necessary quality for successful cause. Such quality was not only trained in class. A successful teacher influenced his students unconsciously and step by step in daily time. A teacher should possess artistic talents of actors in order to become a successful teacher in class. In West Point of U.S., to become a senior general and lead a mighty force, first you needed to have personality charisma and could convince people.

A person with great charms required himself to be a flag, an example and a pacemaker with strong rallying force, appetency, appeal and convincing power. Some students said Yingge was observant and alert in class. His gestures and intonations were permeated with cadence. He always concentrated and students watched him happily as if he was a performing artist. Students could remember what he explained in class without having to review what he taught in class.

Professor Yingge said, "As we see in the movie, Lenin, Sun Yat-sen and Zhou Enlai are the model of personality charisma. Their phenomenal temperament will make you stand in awe as they just stand there, and bring people hope, confidence, courage and strength. Their speeches are born in mind forever."

Yingge had always paid attention to the cultivation of his personality charisma. He always dressed clean with elegant appearance, modesty and prudence, appropriate manners, gentle speech and hospitability on all occasions such as class, meeting, banquet and negation with the outside. Plus, his talents and abilities left people with respectful feelings. All this impressed people in a unique way. It's intangible assets for his success. The alloy research institute led by Yingge had participated in many national large metal surface abrasion-proof project bidding meetings which were even attended by foreigners. Those projects which Yingge participated were all large projects which had higher requirements for technology with certain risks. The gain rate was quite high. Yingge's defense convinced them.

Yingge realized that science and technology competition was becoming the focus of international competition. Nowadays, whoever possessed cutting-edge knowledge and scientific progress advantages would take the initiative in economic development and triumph in the world's science and technology field. We should follow the socialist independent innovation path with Chinese characteristics, start with the demand of economic development, focus on making breakthroughs in key technologies and be listed in the world's advanced science and technology countries.

Yingge often told his students, "To open the door to high technologies in the world, the most important thing is to grasp several foreign languages which are the bridges to success. You might have experienced that learning a foreign language is not easy. You need to make great efforts. In addition to English, we should learn German and Russian...... Ding Zhaozhong, an overseas Chinese in America, was a Noble Prize winner. He succeeded in the neutron experiment in a German laboratory, which shocked the entire world. It could be seen that German technology and scientific experiment methods are quite advanced. Besides, Russian is a necessity as well. Russia's space technology and other scientific fields take the leading position in the world, which is obvious to all."

Yingge educated his students earnestly and tirelessly, "You should learn the second foreign language—German in your spare time. English is the main course so you need to be proficient at it. Once you get the hang of German, it will be easy to learn Russian.

If you can grasp German, Russian and English well, you will lay a solid foundation for mounting science peaks in future."

One time, it's past 10:00pm. Yingge was still making up lessons for students. The rain poured with lightening and thundering. However, he insisted in lecturing for them. The entire building was in darkness. Someone knocked at the door and entered an old guard man who was on night shift, "The school gate is already closed and light turned off. It's time for you to leave for rest."

As the old man prompted, students left the classroom with resignation. Yingge walked the students out of the main gate who asked, "How will you go home since it's raining heavily outside?" Yingge answered, "I will see. I will stay in the classroom for a while if it goes on like this. Nothing to worry about. You go!" Students left. The rain was pouring harder and harder. Yingge couldn't go home and walked back and forth in the classroom to think about that day's lesson. He sat down to read the book and prepare lessons for the next day. He might be so tired after a day's hard work that he fell into sleep over the desk.

4. Necklace Hanging on the Tomb

Yingge had received two letters from Feng Qinqin since he left the Snowy Forest and came to Heilongjiang University.

In the first letter, she told Yingge that she was fine. She was transferred to the lumbering site from the forestry bureau as a statistician as required by the work conditions. She was busy in the mountains. The traffic there was inconvenient and there's no post office so communications was hard and the letter couldn't be received most of the time.

In her second letter, she wished Yingge accomplish both success and fame soon and she was waiting for him.

Yingge often wrote to Feng Qinqin later but didn't receive Feng's reply.

Yingge was in panic, "My love, where are you? Why? Why don't you reply me?"

After asking about her from his friends, he learned that she was transferred to a lumbering camp of a virgin forest in Jilin from Heilongjiang but he didn't know the specific institution. Yingge tried to contact her for several times but failed.

Therefore, Yingge had been restless, with a bee in his head because he knew accidents might happen anytime in the virgin forest like being swallowed by tigers or wolves or lost in the forest, or……

Yingge missed his love day and night, and looked forward to her letter from afar.

Time flied. It had been years in an instant. A number of years later, one day in early spring, Yingge found a letter from Changchun Hospital among a pack of letters from different places which were placed on the sill of the letter office.

Yingge opened the letter immediately to find it's Feng's letter. He's so excited that his heart beat intensely.

Feng apologized to him and introduced her recent conditions in the letter. Her work place had changed frequently. Now she's working in Changbai Mountains Forestry Bureau in Jilin. She had been in poor health and her disease had aggravated year by year. She didn't write to Yingge because she didn't want to affect Yingge's work. She said sorry and asked for his forgiveness.

Feng suffered from liver cancer and was waiting for surgery in Changchun Hospital.

The letter seemed a written death judgment of Feng. Yingge was in extreme agony. Distress and sorrow made him physically and spiritual haggard. They were so far away from each other and they were busy. What should he do? He decided to send her some money first for treatment.

He told his mother that he wanted to send money to Feng for curing her disease. He also explained to his mother about their past and the fond love between them. After hearing what Yingge said, his mother let Yingge send all his salary of the month to Feng.

Since then, Yingge hadn't received any letter from Feng. Yingge couldn't go visit her because his teaching schedule was tight and couldn't leave at all. He had been burning with anxiety. Finally the holidays came. He immediately went to Changchun Hospital and inquired about Feng's work place and address. It turned out that Feng worked in a little village of the forest area in Jilin and lived in two runty houses beside the road.

Yingge went inside the house but he only found a little girl. He wondered why Feng Qinqin was not there. Later he learned that the little girl was her adopted daughter named Little Honghong. Her parents had died of acute diseases and nobody took care of her so Feng took her in out of sympathy.

Little Honghong told Yingge about her mother's past: Feng didn't get married but raised her up. Feng often mentioned Yingge, "He is a teacher in a university and he's a very excellent person. I haven't met and wrote to him for years."

Little Honghong continued with tears in her eyes. Feng Qinqin often wept and said she had been grateful to Yingge in her lifetime and couldn't return him for saving her life. Yingge's love for her was the greatest. However, she couldn't repay him anymore and then she would start sobbing. As Little Honghong recalled, she couldn't help crying.

Feng told Little Honghong that it's Yingge who saved her from the wild wolves in the forest area. At that time, Yingge left the death to himself and asked her to run.

Feng also said, "How terrible it was at that moment!" Feng cried and narrated her narrow escape story.

In the end, Little Honghong led Uncle Yingge to the tomb of Feng.

Yingge took off his hat and stood in front of Feng's tombstone silently. He was so painful that he wept sad and anguish tears. The huge pain on the inside made him speechless. His dream of getting married with her was gone….. He fished out a shining gold necklace from his pocket and hung it on the tomb of Feng with full respect so as to express his loyalty to her and show the eternity of love. At the same time, he lost control and cried out loud, "Ah! Qinqin, if you are standing in front of me, I will wear the necklace for you in person. How happy we would be! But I couldn't see you anymore. I didn't think you would leave so early that you couldn't witness my success and fame."

Yingge found it hard to believe the truth that they couldn't see each other anymore. However, for years he had been waiting for her.

He was waiting for her when he felt frustrated and desperate in autumn rains.

He was waiting for her when others thought it's impossible for them to meet each other.

He was waiting for her when there's no reply as time passed by.

He was waiting for her when he stood at the seashore, stared at the sailboat going afar and imagined it could return as it thundered and stormed.

He was still waiting for her when friends persuaded him not to entertain any expectation and illusion.

Yingge gave some money to Little Honghong when he left and asked her to buy some flowers for Feng whenever she went to her tomb, thus showing his permanent condolence for her. Besides, part of the money was for Little Honghong's living expenses. Little Honghong pulled Yingge's clothes, reluctant to let him leave.

Yingge bid farewell to Feng and left the most precious "footprint" of love.

5. Love of Blood between Yingge and His Student

For years of teaching and educating his students, Yingge had been sticking to the principle of "persuading and convincing people both sentimentally and rationally".

Yingge was selfless to his students with his fatherly care and profound love of blood. Professor Yingge had a unique temperament. From his inner side to outside, he naturally expressed his deep love for his students and had common potential qualities possessed by all other excellent teachers. His conducts and smile made him look like a father to students. He treated his students as his sons while being tireless in teaching. In front of students, he's not only a teacher but also a father who's profoundly respected and admired by students. In his career course, what he thought most was two words: student and talent for which he had contributed his lifetime. He was thinking about how to train students into talents and train excellent students into high-end talents all the time.

With a down-to-earth academic attitude, he trained and cared about his students, and often invited needy students home for visit.

One day, when he was lecturing, he found that Wu Qiao was absent. Later he learned that she was hospitalized in Bincheng

Infectious Disease Hospital. After class, Yingge directly went to the suburb hospital on his bicycle.

Yingge explained why he came to the nurse on shift, "I am Wu Qiao's teacher and come to see her."

The nurse said, "What Wu Qiao suffered is severe tuberculosis and high fever as well. It's the open infection period so he must be separated for treatment. No families are allowed to see her. It might take several months."

Yingge laughed loudly, "I have experienced a lot of narrow escapes. I have been in an environment with tigers, wild boars and wolves for several years and I still survived. Tuberculosis is nothing to me. I have great immune competence so I am not afraid of it."

The nurse stared at Yingge with surprise, "Is there such kind of person who's not afraid of anything including death in the world?"

After repeated requests of Yingge, the nurse had to give in and told Yingge not to stay too long. Yingge entered No. 303 ward and saw Wu Qiao was leaning against the bed. She looked emaciated and kept coughing like a frosted flower after autumn. She raised her head with lassitude.

Wu Qiao was both happy and anxious to see her teacher. Out of respect and love for her teacher, she said instinctively, "I am having an infectious disease and the doctor doesn't allow any relative to visit me. Besides, I missed too many classes and I don't think I can catch up so I feel a lot of pressure. I don't think I can step it up anymore."

Wu Qiao said, "I was born in a poor village and now the infectious disease is killing me. My family can't afford my study anymore. I will drop out after being discharged from the hospital. I can't study anymore and I will go farming at home. So I don't want to make up my lessons. Thank you for your good intention! I will be sad if I spread the disease to you. Please go back."

Yingge cordially encouraged, "You must insist in studying and can't give up. I can help you with your difficulties. You are a junior now and will graduate in one year. You have been trained for a dozen of years so you shouldn't give up. You must stick to it. Don't worry about the lessons. I will make them up for you. I will also try my best to help you with your tuition and daily life. Hang in there and try to become a successful graduate." Wu Qiao was moved to tears by Yingge's words.

Yingge said, "Considering your current situation, both teachers and the university have the responsibility to help you. Life is not always rosy but permeated with high tides and low ebbs. As long as the university and teachers support you, you just be relaxed and receive the treatment. Soon you will be kicking your heels again." Yingge's words convinced Wu Qiao who revealed her long-time-no-see smiles.

Wu Qiao said, "I will do what you told me." Yingge said, "There you go."

Yingge came to teach Wu Qiao in the hospital twice a week. Yingge clarified the contents, sorted out key points and explained difficult points with concise language and cordial tones. Through over a month's teaching, the lessons she missed were almost made up.

Yingge also explained many philosophies of life to Wu Qiao, encouraged her to get better soon and return to the university for study.

Yingge continued, "I have survived at crucial junctures, and met a lot more difficulties than you did. I even didn't think I would live until today. I hope students I train can become excellent talents after graduation, achieve academic success with learned knowledge, be brave to innovate, set pioneering example, grasp more knowledge to repay society. It's my standard of training talents, that is, be a person who contributes to his country and people. "

Yingge's words were just like a key which opened Wu Qiao's heart and let her bounce back again. She's happy so she would recover more quickly. She wanted Yingge to teach her now. Yingge taught her like this for several weeks. She decided to act like Yingge and feared no dangers and difficulties. She studied and tried to become a useful talent while being treated in the hospital.

In his second visit, Yingge brought her some money for food and some nutritious food.

With the instruction and help of Yingge, Wu Qiao was soon discharged from the hospital and went back to the campus to study in the class.

Yingge told her, "I will do my best to help you with your future life and study. You must go it through to graduation. Everything will be better."

With the help of Yingge and through her own unremitting efforts, Wu Qiao gained the title of Excellent Student when she graduated and was sent to work in Northern Locomotive Factory. Wu Qiao worked and studied hard at work and tried to apply what she learned in college to production practices. She had made constant great performances and contributed to the company so she became a well-known technician in the factory and the inviting professor of the group company.

Several years later, at a national high-tech seminar, Wu Qiao and academician Yingge came across each other in the hall. Wu Qiao recognized her respected teacher Yingge at the first sight. She shouted, "Teacher! You are also here." Yingge had taught too many students so he was stupefied for an instant after hearing "teacher", "You are......" Lots of changes had happened in the past years so Yingge found it hard to recognize her.

"I am your student Wu Qiao. You went to the hospital to make up lessons for me before." Wu Qiao was excited. It suddenly reminded Yingge of the love of blood between them.

Wu Qiao introduced her work and life conditions after graduation to Yingge.

Wu Qiao didn't forget her teacher's instructions after graduation and didn't fail the Party's years of training. She served as a professor-level and senior engineer of the group company through hard working in the science field who's entitled to special expert allowances. Besides, she worked as the chief engineer of the group's latest super-high-speed locomotive, had gone to foreign countries for technical exchanges and seminars for several times, thus having made immense contributions to the development of China's high-speed electric locomotives.

Wu Qiao said to her teacher with emotions, "I wouldn't be what I am today but for your training, instructions and help with my daily life. You are the benefactor of my entire lifetime. I am finally a useful person to our country now."

Yingge said, "I am so happy that we meet each other today. It's destined between us. I happed to have a invention patent. I need you such computer expert and master like you to help me do the designs. Hopefully we can become technical cooperation partners and let us join hands to make more contributions to the construction of our motherland!"

6. Seminar about Training of Science Masters

At a national seminar, how to train science masters was discussed. The leader asked Yingge to make an excellent speech, "How to train contemporary undergraduates into masters is a compelling topic which should attracts the attention of the public especially the educators. As an educator myself, I would like to talk about my opinions based on my experience of being trained in Heilongjiang University so as to start our discussion. I am very glad to discuss such an important topic with new and old educators, professors and doctors present to speed up the talent training in colleges and universities."

Yingge said enthusiastically, "An innovative and socialist country with Chinese characteristics should be built under the instructions of the scientific outlook on development. It makes it clear that colleges and universities should train a great batch of independently innovative talents for the country who will become international science masters and leading roles in the science and technology teams such as experts in the exploration of the universe and space; experts in national defense high-tech construction; experts in exploration of human beings' health and longevity and experts in elimination of the dangers of air pollution to human beings."

At the meeting, Dr. Wang Kai, graduate of German RWTH Aachen University, asked, "Mr. Yingge, what conditions are required for training high-level talents?"

Yingge said, "As the ancient saying goes, 'Practice is better than precept.' As educators, first, we should be fully confident, seize opportunities and take the lead to work out new innovations. Besides, we should study and develop new technological projects in our own science systems and fields, direct students to look for topics in production practices, apply theories to practices, let our students rank among the world's high technologies and experience new innovation breakthroughs, train their spirit of mounting science peaks, and enable them to take risks and forge ahead with determination in scientific researches. For example, the newspaper reported that a twenty-year-old young student was assessed as a university professor, which proved that 'swift horses' indeed exist among Chinese undergraduates."

Professor Wang Li who once studied in Oxford University of Britain asked, "Our government wants to build an innovative country. So how should we deal with its relationship between the current policies of introducing technologies and talents from the outside and to the outside?"

Yingge answered, "The world's scientific development practices tell us that only when a country has strong independent innovation ability can it seize the opportunity and win initiative amid intense international competition. In particular, in terms of those key crucial technologies influencing China's national defense safety and economic development, we can't just depend on introduction. For example, we wanted to import the space suits for spacemen in 'Shenzhou VII' because we had difficulty in manufacturing them but failed. Later on, Russia provided two space suits for us to show their support for our aerospace cause. Aviation and space technologies must rely on independent innovation. We must have the ability and courage to overcome key technologies needed by the country. Now our scientists have overcome many aviation and space technological problems which can't be solved in the past."

Professor Ma Lin who studied at Harvard University of U.S. posed a question, "We are trying to tackle cutting-edge technologies. However, our laboratory equipments are not improved yet and there's still difficulty. What should we do?"

Yingge said, "Please forgive me. I don't like hearing the word of 'difficulty'. Independent innovation itself brings with it difficulties. It is because of difficulties that we are here to address them and work hard. We must make innovations no matter what the external environment is. If we don't have such perseverance and the great spirit of fighting and climbing, we won't be able to reach the science peaks, let alone the training of excellent students and science masters. There's no free lunch in the world neither can we succeed overnight. Scientific research success requires plenty of blood and efforts as well as dedication spirit."

Dr. Zhao Lin, an overseas student from Moscow State University, asked, "Lack of funds in scientific researches over the years has influenced the progress of independent innovation. What do you think of the problem?"

Yingge answered, "I appreciate the frankness of Dr. Zhao. Marxists maintain that material is the most important thing. It's hard to do anything without funds because financial support is the basis, which is a fact. However, where there's a will, there's a way. We can find it from knowledge, textbooks and practices. College and universities collect plenty of graduation papers every year especially theses for master's degree and dissertations for doctor's degree. What are these papers for? Aren't these high-level illustrations and exploration in the fields instructive to economic construction? Can't they be turned into productivity? Aren't technical transfers made? What's the value of these papers if they can't serve productivity? Are we just playing with words? My graduation paper in Heilongjiang University was adopted by the company and the technical transfer was worth hundreds of thousands of yuan which was all donated to Heilongjiang University for scientific research funds. Why can't we make technical transfers? Why can't they be applied in enterprises?"

"If these papers can start with and come from production practices, and then be applied in production practices to contribute to productivity development, aren't they valuable? Aren't they the sources of scientific research funds? Such papers are valuable. Such doctors are innovative doctors. We can't just leave for home after wearing the doctorial hat and the academician tag."

Yingge wrapped up his speech, "Our training goal, be them bachelor's degree, master's degree, doctor's degree or science masters, is to train innovative talents for national economic construction and the development of advanced productivity. Only such talents can have their capabilities demonstrated in this innovative country. Only such talents are real scientists, science masters and academicians. For instance, Mr. Yuan Longping, father of hybrid rice in China and even the world, has been fighting in the rice fields for dozens of years. In order to solve the food problem of China's huge population, he had worked hard in arduous environment for years without complaining, and finally succeeded in producing 900 to 1,000 kilos of hybrid rice for each mu. It shocked the entire world and it far exceeded some countries with developed sciences in the world. Academician Yuan Longping is the goal for us to train masters in future."

Yingge's speech won warm applause!

7. Oral Defense for Doctoral Dissertation

The announcement for the graduation dissertation oral defense of Ma Chao, an excellent student representative trained by Yingge was posted on the bulletin board in front of the university gate.

Doctoral dissertation topic "Exploration of 'Robot' Applied in the New Technology of High Temperature Boiler Spray and Wear-resisting Alloy"

Venue: Defense Hall of College of Metal Material Technology

Date: August 8, 1996

Respondent: Ma Chao from School of Metal Surface Engineering

Supervisor: Associate Professor Yingge from School of Arts and Science

Students and teachers of the university are welcome to participate and offer instructions.

August 1, 1996

Students and teachers swarmed in front of the bulletin board. They were having a hot discussion. Some of them were surprised, some envied, some commented and some doubted......

Someone said, "It's only a paper of an undergraduate which is just a summarization report. The teacher gives a topic and students can finish it by copying here and there, and drawing several drafts. After that they can graduate. I have never heard that an undergraduate dare participate in a doctoral dissertation oral defense. It's purely unbelievable."

Another person said, "He's just genius or superman or super-talent. I won't miss it for the world......" Someone exclaimed, "He's the hero of undergraduates!" Someone discussed, "Robots can freely operate the spray just like people do? They can move up and down, left to right, back and forth, with concision and flexibility. The technology is really advanced and the latest technology in modern spray field. It sets a pioneering example in Chinese and foreign spray technology fields. It's amazing and admirable!"

A teacher introduced, "The spray by robots requires high-level automation technology, remote control technology, precise processing technology, digital technology, computer technology, material science technology and supersonic-speed spray technology. It's a cutting-edge technology both home and abroad. Our university should feel considerably glorious and proud for training such great talents."

Another teacher said, "It's over 40 meters in the large power generation boiler. The environment inside the boiler is really bad with too many dusts, high temperature and heavy pollution. Can the robot bear all of this? It's too difficult and requires advanced technologies."

Mr. Niu Hai stood aside. With a large head and big ears, he's short and fat, and wore a pair of glasses. He squinted his small eyes and gestured to make irresponsible remarks. He was not convinced because his eyes showed contempt. He disdained, "Mr. Yingge is an associate professor himself. How come he can train a doctor? It's a legend but also a joke. Can monkeys train elephants? Can ants surpass the airplane? Can pupils become academicians?" His words triggered a burst of laughters. He even instigated, "It's impossible! Ants are just ants. They are not elephants. Do you ever hear of such joke like mosquitoes being faster than rockets. I have never heard of it. They are just bragging and talking nonsense. I bet the oral defense will definitely screw up. Let's wait and see."

Niu Hai was slack and perfunctory at ordinary times. He's not so well educate but his words were weird so students were not satisfied with him. He said so many unpractical words without any scruple which caused aversion and resistance of students present. Two students dealt him a blow straight forward without thinking about the teacher-student relationship. He's speechless and red-faced. He squeezed out of the crowd and tried to slip away with embarrassment.

A student standing beside him asked, ill-affected, "Mr. Niu, do you know practice is the only standard to test the truth? How do you know it won't work since you haven't participated the oral defense? Isn't possible to have genius and excellent students among us? In my opinion, teachers might be lousy and students can be genius. The worthy disciple excels his masters! Do you agree with me? Besides, as a teacher, you should have a teacher's ethics and shoulder responsibilities. How many excellent students have you trained? You should be proud and happy for such excellent students trained in our university. You can't look down upon our classmates!"

Another student retorted, "I heard that Mr. Niu wanted to become an associate professor but foreign language level was required. You dared not sign up for the exam, complained and shouted, 'it's illegal to take the exam for teachers. It seems that foreign language shouldn't be tested for being a teacher. Even a person who can't understand a foreign language can still be a professor.' Didn't you say so? And you didn't dare to take the exam anyway. However, teacher Yingge went there and achieved good performance so he is an associate professor. How do you explain this? He has trained an excellent student to take part in the doctoral dissertation oral defense. What about you? Please don't talk about anything bad about others here and there."

Niu Hai glared at the student with his little eyes, "You don't respect your teacher. It's none of your business whether I know foreign language or not. It's just nonsense." People laughed. He was red-faced and escaped from the crowd, with his tail between his legs.

After long preparation, the oral defense meeting was held as scheduled and the hall was packed with people. Some people even stood in the corridor. People present included professors, leaders, students and overseas students, etc.

Professor Mu Shan, the host of the meeting and academic dean of Jiaotong University, announced that the meeting opened. Professor Mu Shan was a senior leader of the university who dared to speak, act and innovate. In addition to his deep attainments in locomotive studies, he drove the train and created many new majors and new teaching & research offices. For example, the Second Foreign Language Teaching & Research Office (German, Russian, French and Japanese) was established by him. Multiple foreign language teaching was set up for postgraduates, undergraduates and overseas students of the university, which was the first example among the country's engineering colleges and universities.

Professor Mu Shan announced, "Today's oral defense meeting is of special significance. It's the first time Jiaotong University holds such a meeting. With the Party's training and instructions of his supervisor Yingge, Ma Chao is going to participate in the doctoral dissertation oral defense as an undergraduate, which is an exception. The oral defense is unprecedented. In order to hold a successful meeting, our university invites Professor Liu Zhongmin, doctoral supervisor and vice president of Huaqing University, Professor Cheng Qiuyuan, vice president of Dalian University Science & Engineering and academician of Chinese Academy of Sciences, Researcher Zhang Shiping from Physical Chemistry Research Institute of Chinese Academy of Sciences, Dr. Hill, a German expert in Chinese

Automation Study Science Institute, and Professor Chen and Professor Li, doctoral supervisors of Robot Research Institute of Beijing Aerospace University, academicians of Chinese Academy of Engineering, and academicians of WAPS. We are honored to have the British expert Professor Hill present at the meeting. Let's welcome him." (Thundering applause heard)

Professor Mu Shan continued, "Led by the Party, our university has followed the road of reform and opening-up. We have trained talents without sticking to one pattern only. Ma Chao is a typical representative. Associate professor Yingge has spent a lot of painstaking efforts to train an undergraduate into a talent who can write a doctoral dissertation. It's a miracle of the education field. He is courageous to explore and innovate while educating students. His achievements result from dozens of times of meticulous and hard experiments. They have overcome difficulties in the past few bitter winters and hot summers. They are diligent and dedicated, have consulted with several experts and professors of colleges and universities as well as senior engineers in large enterprises, studied multiple technologies such as machine principles, automation technology, remote control technology, digital meter technology, electricity and supersonic spray technology. What's more precious is that Ma Chao presents a design which meets the production demands and has been transformed to productivity, thus creating great wealth for the country. Next let's invite Ma Chao to report his study process about the topic."

Ma Chao walked fast to the platform and started, "The invention and application of robots belong to a cutting-edge technology both home and abroad today. It's a new technology. Now I would like to play a video of how robots work to let you see the difference between the new and old technologies. Then you will understand the scientific value of my paper."

Yingge thought Ma Chao's opening speech was appropriate and awesome. His throbbing heart turned tranquil a bit.

At the oral defense meeting, Yingge's watched every word, every conduct and every move of Ma Chao like a father. Ma Chao was a top student whom he had spared no effort to train in the past few years. Ma Chao's success was the success in Yingge's teaching.

Ma Chao turned on the TV set and the old spray technology appeared on the screen. Manual operation was conducted in the old technology. The smoke in the boiler was dense with vague vision so it caused severe harm to workers' health. The spray effects can't be guaranteed. What's more, a team of three people was required for the operation. The conditions were bad, the work was difficult and the progress was slow.

Ma Chao pressed the screen and the scene of robot operation showed up. A person in white overall was operating the computer buttons outside the boiler. The robot was operating according to the automatic program in the boiler. It climbed up and down, right to left, and was working in order, thus producing even layers, solid alloy structure and clean surfaces. There was little smoke in the boiler which was clean and bright with standard sizes. Everyone was watching it like a fantasy film. They were so surprised and excited that they applauded hard.

Professor Mu Shan said, "Next the oral defense starts."

Professor Wang asked first, "Ma Chao, can you explain the features of high temperature wear-resisting and high impact wear-resisting? What are the respective advantages of manual operation and robot operation?"

Ma Chao answered with full confidence, "Thank you, Professor! There's a danger in high impact wear-resisting during the manual operation. At the first time when the teacher instructed us to do the experiment, I was careless and didn't operate according to the operation rules. The strong laser electric arc sent by the laser bar suddenly hit the teacher's eyes, which was extremely dangerous. Our experiment site was a large power generation plant in a remote mountain village where the impact wear-resisting studies were made. Professor Yingge was injured by the high-pressure laser arc and he was so painful that he rolled on the floor. But there's no large hospital in the local place. I didn't protect my teacher and it's caused by my carelessness. I was so sad, anguish and guilty, which made me restless. I cried to the teacher, 'what to do? Where can we see a doctor late at night? The teacher comforted me with extreme pain, 'I can hold on. Let's go to the hospital tomorrow! Don't be sad. It's my fault as well. I didn't remind you enough."

Ma Chao continued, "A fall into the pit, a gain in your wit. Something bad might turn into something good. The teacher's wound was caused by me. I am so sorry for that. I decided to improve the 'robot'. Later on, the 'robot' can be eventually used to replace the manual impact-proof and wear-resisting work. The use of 'robot' is not only safe and efficient but also reliable in quality."

Then Ma Chao demonstrated the impact-proof and wear-resisting work operated by the robot to people. With the screen turned on, people could see the robot was operating in an orderly way under the strong arc. Workers were far away from "robots". The screen showed that the robots had replaced manual labor, which was safe. Moreover, the impact and wear-resisting strength was over 10 times greater. It's alloy so it wouldn't be damaged no matter how strong the impact force was. "Let's take a look at how robots operate in the large power generation boiler. All programs are back-fed to the computer through the camera. Then the computer buttons are controlled by people. You can observe the work conditions of the robot in the boiler through the screen. The robot is very obedient and can follow any order of human beings."

"I am a journalist from East Wind Daily. Are such technology and process introduced before home and abroad?"

"As far as I am concerned, the answer is no."

"If not, I suggest you apply for a foreign patent and publish it as soon as possible to secure the world's science and technology front."

Professor Wang said with appreciation, "The journalist's suggestion is quite right. We should release it first and obtain the world's markets."

Academician Cheng Qiuyuan from Dalian University of Science & Engineering asked, "I have no question to ask. The performance on the screen has proved everything. The robot spray is very successful. Practice is the criterion for testing all the truths. It's an independent and innovative technology. I just want to say something. Today, I have learned a lot from Ma Chao's doctoral dissertation oral defense. No undergraduate participated in the doctoral dissertation oral defense in our university. We should learn from Jiaotong University. It's another abundant achievement in the education field. I agree with Professor Wang's opinion that Ma Chao's paper should be released as soon as possible. It also provides enlightenment for other undergraduates."

Professor Liu Zhongmin from Huaqing University showed his care, "I will go for Professor Cheng's opinion. The fact that an undergraduate takes part in the doctoral dissertation oral defense really inspires us. I think in future we need to teach students in accordance with their aptitude. Some undergraduates' papers are also excellent so we can train them without sticking to one pattern only. I also think his paper should be published in the world as soon as possible. He should apply for the world invention patent to prove that China's science and technology are advanced, Chinese students are gifted, Chinese scientists are capable of outstanding achievements and Chinese advanced education system can train talents."

Niu Hai stood up suddenly and asked with disdain, "Ma Chao, I have a small question. 'Robot' is a high technology which is not the project of undergraduates. It's a comprehensive high technology. Do you copy it somewhere? Or do you copy it from foreign journals?"

Ma Chao was indignant but he said calmly, "There's a clean answer to your question, Mr. Niu. Since it hasn't been put on production in foreign countries, how can I copy? How can I copy from something that doesn't exist? Therefore, your question is not appropriate. You can't just doubt randomly. It's not serious to propose a question which is groundless."

Niu Hai flushed with shame and left the meeting, crestfallen.

The oral defense continued.

Professor Wang asked again, "Ma Chao, the 'robot' and spray technologies are a comprehensive cutting-edge science. How did you grasp these sciences?"

Ma Chao looked at Yingge with emotions. It seemed that there's something which couldn't be expressed. Yingge felt relieved and proud for Ma Chao. Ma Chao admired and was grateful to Yingge. He was greatly encouraged by his teacher's eyes. He said, "My paper has been written with the instructions of my supervisor Yingge and through consultations with quite a few experts and professors of our university. I learned from the textbooks in class and in the factories outside as well as technical experts in research institutes. I have walked so far step by step. I am standing on the shoulders of Yingge and other teachers. So to speak, without them, I wouldn't have made today's achievements. One should never forget where one's happiness comes from. My supervisor Yingge has put a lot of blood to train me into an undergraduate who grasps inter-disciplinary knowledge. My paper covers multiple boundary sciences such as theoretical mechanics, applied physics, chemistry, electrotechnics, automatic control, computer software remote control technology, feedback technology, supersonic speed metal surface treatment, power generation boiler, heat transfer theory and arc supersonic spray technology. Hence, I can grasp so much knowledge because professors of different fields have spared no effort to teach me. Here I would like to extend my sincere gratitude to my supervisor Yingge for his tireless teaching. Because of him, I can stand on this platform today. Besides, my thanks also go to other professors in addition to my supervisor, the Party Committee of Dalian Jiaotong University and the university leaders for their training and education. The love of Professor Yingge is like that of my parents. No matter how tall a tree grows, it will never forget its root. And even if a teacher has taught me for one day, I will treat him like my father."

The host academic dean Mu Shan announced: Next let's welcome Professor Wang to comment.

Professor Wang said happily, "I think today's oral defense meeting is quite successful. Mr. Niu Hai is the only person who has an opposite opinion. In my opinion, as an academic researcher, we should listen to both positive and negative ones. However, we should analyze them. If there's something to improve, we will do that. If not, we can use it to remind us not to make that mistake."

"Besides, you have proposed lots of opinions and questions today. Ma Chao has answered them. As to the issue of securing the world's high-tech field, we must release it first before western countries do. It's very important. Ma Chao should be well prepared and submit relevant materials."

Professor Liu Zhongmin from Huaqing University approved as well, "I can't agree with Professor Wang anymore. Such high-tech achievement must be published first to let western countries witness the doctoral level of our undergraduates. He has greatly encouraged and inspired Chinese undergraduates. I would like to officially invite Professor Yingge and Ma Chao to do an academic report in Huaqing University."

Ma Chao said affectionately, "Both Professor Wang Professor Liu agree that I should have it published first but I want to talk about a practical problem. My supervisor Yingge was an associate professor at present. The title hasn't been reviewed for over a decade. My supervisor Yingge possesses super advanced mode of thinking and has given me great instructions. His erudite knowledge and dialectical recognition will be the learning example in my lifetime. He's worth my respect and admiration. He has repeatedly educated us that we shouldn't emphasize fame and wealth; instead we should focus on true skills and genuine knowledge. We should compare contributions, knowledge and whether we can transform our knowledge into productivity to be used in our motherland's construction. He pays little attention to titles, fame and wealth in daily time. Therefore, Yingge teacher should be promoted to professor. Only in this way can the release of this paper be perfectly justifiable. The signature should be Professor Yingge. Only in this way can it show its importance. Further, I won't feel guilty and won't be commented irresponsibly. I can't just forget my teacher after I make some achievements." Speaking of this, Ma Chao wept. "Hence, I won't have my paper published unless my supervisor Yingge is addressed as professor. I would like to ask the university leaders' approval. It's not accidental that I can stand here to answer your questions but because Yingge teacher has made great efforts to train me. Mr. Yingge has taught many postgraduates who have become great talents after graduation."

Professor Wang was so moved, "Ma Chao's profound love for Yingge is a model for student-teacher relationships and worth carrying forward. It's Chinese people's tradition to be grateful. No matter how tall a tree grows, it won't forget its root. Teachers and students should bear sincere emotions. As to the issue of promoting Yingge to a professor, the university's title evaluation committee needs to discuss it."

Secretary Li Ming chipped in, "Comrade Yingge, supervisor of Ma Chao was the chairman of the trade union of School of Arts and Science. He has strong gifts for arts and sports, mobilization ability and organization ability. "

"He's a qualified supervisor. He comes to tutor his students, look up in foreign materials and help students solve learning difficulties no matter it's hot summer or bitter winter, holidays or working days."

"Ma Chao stands out because Yingge has trained him with painstaking efforts for years……"

Ma Chao interposed, “I respect Secretary Li Ming. He’s a good leader who dares to speak and act, emphasizes practices and talents with a dauntless and unyielding spirit.”

The paper of “The Application of Robots in Metal Surface Wear-resisting Technology” was soon published in a world’s science & technology magazine after discussion, and caused a sensation in the world’s science & technology field. Scientific research organizations of many countries wrote to extend their congratulations. Many enterprises wanted to buy the patented technology and scholars came to visit Jiaotong University in an endless stream so the fame of Jiaotong University would be improved rapidly. They had made academic reports successively in famous domestic and foreign universities. In addition, they absorbed the experience of other universities, conducted academic exchanges and became the envoys of academic exchanges among colleges and universities.

Part V Second Golden Age

1. Scientific Researches Should Serve Productivity

Time sped past and it's already earlier 1990s. Yingge left his beloved rostrum. He's still meditating and exploring another turning of his life. He still desired for improving and meeting new challenges, thus transcending the first golden age.

China was poor at that time. What's worse it just underwent a catastrophe. Chinese nation lagged behind among the world's nations, especially western capitalist countries. Were people of a country with over one billion of population and ancient civilization reconciled? People were racking their brains: China must revitalize but how? With the leadership of the Party, Deng Xiaoping, chief designer of socialist with Chinese characteristics secured the commanding height and proposed that we should show respect for knowledge and talents; science and technology were the primary productive forces; we should revitalize our country through science and technology as well as reform and opening-up.

Yingge thought retirement period was the beginning of his second golden age. It's the perfect time to demonstrate his talents with his rich experience, mature technologies, great personality charisma, agile thinking and comprehensive technology spread.

Yingge was really sagacious. At key moments, he went with the times and insisted his choice. Under the support of the municipal science committee and Jiaotong University, Yingge established Jiaotong University Dalian Kathrin Special Alloy Research Institute to be engaged in scientific research innovation, corporate management and technical inventions. It's the only "right way" to combine theories with practices and let scientific researches serve productivity.

Economic benefits were stressed for scientific researches and corporate management. There's no vitality without benefits. Scientific research achievements were the watershed for identifying whether a country was strong or weak. Where did benefits come from? He must throw off his professor airs, learn from founders of small and medium-sized enterprises, study the markets and obtain benefits from markets. Only in this way could scientific research achievements be connected with production practices and transformed to strong productivity. Whether they can be turned into productivity was the touchstone for identifying those achievements and the only way of experts who studied engineering. On the road of scientific research, Yingge had undergone vicissitudes and passed over twenty springs and autumns with down-to-earth "footprints".

The first step was always the hardest to make. It's more so for Yingge. At the inception of the research institute, he started from scratch so scientific researches were stuck in difficulties: no capital, no equipment, no factory and no laboratory. It's hard for common people to overcome such difficulties.

Yingge regarded difficulty as a spring. When you went hard, it would become soft; when you went soft, it would be hard. To be hard, one must have money. Everything was out of the question without money. In order to raise money, he bit the bullet to borrow from others, loan and sell his assets such as camera, bicycles, color TV and other valuable things. Finally he had the start-up capital and registration capital prepared.

The research institute finally opened but where were the markets? Where to start with? It's a strategic problem in corporate management. China's ancient Master Sun's Art of War stressed, "Knowing the enemy and yourself, you can fight a hundred battles and win them all" and "Avoid the strong and attack the weak; attack the weak points with strong points". As long as one followed the rule, one could win the war. Yingge asked himself whether he had certain technical strength. Through many years' technical studies and exploration on site, Yingge found a way out in the metal surface wear-resisting field.

At that time, large state-owned enterprises had strong technical strength and advanced equipments. Yingge chose not to compete with them and temporarily avoid these enterprises with strong capital. Small and medium-sized enterprises, especially the newly established township enterprises scattered all over the place under the situation of reform and opening-up such as brick factories, small concrete factories, fire-proof material factories and small electricity plants needed mud, stones, sand and coals. Their machinery spare parts were worn in a short time and their wasted steel equipment were piled up, which directly affected production development and improvement of economic benefits. Their technical strength was weak but they had great requirements for technologies. They tried to look for technologies and talents here and there so they welcomed Yingge and his teams to take charge of their technical services and serve as consultants. This was a good strategic opportunity of "avoiding the strong and attacking the weak".

They made countless studies and experiments, referred to science and technology materials of Germany and other countries, and finally succeeded in producing a kind of high strength wear-resisting surfacing material, high temperature laser spray welding alloy powder block and high temperature wear-resisting alloy powder. With the features of high manganese steel including great hardness, good tenacity and low price, and the adoption of special technologies, high temperature flame welding and high temperature laser carbon arc technology spray, they were applied on the spare parts surfaces which were severely damaged in brick, concrete and power generation factories. Through a series of strengthened processes, it's surprisingly found in the production practices that the service life of the equipment was improved by over five times; besides, the product quality was greatly increased as well while the cost was reduced. They were well reviewed among users. It's a victory in the first battle.

Yingge's research institute finally had a market with which wealth came. Although the profit was not abundant, they earned anyway. Then more and more factories came to the research institute to buy materials, wear-resisting welding rods and alloy powder blocks. More and more enterprises invited the technicians of the research institute to provide services on site. The research institute soon addressed their dilemma. Yingge's innovative technologies became useful. He tasted the sweetness of transforming scientific research achievements into productivity. The capital laid a physical foundation for further development and innovations. Finally they became familiar with the strategy of "avoiding the strong and attacking the weak".

Professor Yingge imparted the innovative technology to his students and young workers, trained their hands-on ability and the spirit of standing hardships. He lived, ate and labored with his students, and taught them with both words and deeds in the hopes that they could become useful personnel as soon as possible and innovate in practices.

In a large concrete factory in the suburb, Professor Yingge led the team of five students himself to conduct high energy and high temperature wear-resisting experiments with high temperature laser rods. The new technology was pioneering both home and abroad at that time, and it was a high technology used to serve township enterprises. It's well received among small and medium-sized enterprises as well as township enterprises. Resistance to high temperature, impact and wear is a successful invention patent.

A misfortune happened in that experiment. Too many cooks spoil the broth. A student opened the high voltage power before Professor Yingge wore the high temperature eye-shield. The high-energy laser and carbon arc high temperature converged and produced an arc light that was over 5,000°C and injured Professor Yingge's eyes instantly. His eyes couldn't see anything after the strong light hit him. He covered his eyes with his hands and he felt so painful. It was night and moreover, it's far from the city so they couldn't go to the hospital right away. The students helped their teacher to the bed. Yingge rolled back and forth, and even fell onto the floor. He could hardly bear the pain. The student was so guilty to make his teacher suffer that he cried...... His carelessness brought about such great pains to his teacher. Professor Yingge endured the huge pain and comforted his student, "Don't cry. Don't be sad. You didn't do it on purpose...... It's my fault as well. I didn't remind you. There's no smooth road to scientific research success. Misfortunes and even death might happen anytime. You should be strong and have the spirit of laying your lives for science if necessary. Then you are my good students." In order to let students calm down and be strong, Yingge told those words while suffering great pains. Students stopped crying and

admired their teacher more. Yingge still comforted his students although he's so painful. How could students not respect their teacher? Late at night, Yingge had a high fever and it's very dangerous. He felt powerless and said to his students in a low voice, "It seems that I can't wait until dawn. I am so anguish and find it hard to breathe. If I die, tell my families not to be sad. People die anyway. Don't be sad. Children are still young. I feel content as long as they are trained into talents!" students cried again...... Because of the huge pain, Yingge might have a heart failure. At that time, there's no vehicle in the factory to send Yingge to the hospital.

Professor Yingge had a sleepless night. His eyes were more swollen. The high fever made it harder to breathe. He took out a thick silver needle from his pocket and ground his teeth to penetrate the thick needles into the two acupoints of "Qu Ze" and "Chi Ze" on his left elbow. Lots of blood was bled. Then he penetrated the acupoint of "He Gu". After a while, his body temperature started decreasing and his headache was not that severe. He carried it through to eight in the morning. He finally survived. It's said that Yingge studied acupuncture of traditional Chinese medicine. Everywhere he went, he brought with him different sizes of silver needles in case of emergency. Director Guan of the concrete factory came to visit Professor Yingge at the time he got to work. Seeing he's severely injured, he had Yingge sent to the county hospital with the factory's vehicle. He went through an electrocardiogram the moment he arrived at the hospital. His heartbeat was weak with severe congestive heart failure. The doctor blamed, "Why was sent here so late? If it's a bit later, his life would be endangered. We need to have an emergency rescue......" Through the doctor's hard-working rescue and over 20 days' meticulous treatment and Yingge's patient cooperation, he could finally open his eyes. His blood pressure re-bounced and the heart failure was gradually removed. Professor Yingge had another narrow escape! How terrible it was! He felt extremely happy, "I escaped from death again. I could stand on my feet again." Yingge gradually rehabilitated. After being discharged from the hospital, Yingge proceeded without hesitation and led his students to be devoted into his beloved metal surface wear-resisting project research. In order to transform scientific research achievements into productivity, he had made countless innovations and improvements. It's regarded by manufacturers as economic, practical and reliable. The wear-resisting performance of its equipment could be improved by over five times. A national patent had been applied for the technology with a number of ZL94222154.0. In order to promote the new technology and employ engineer, technicians and higher-level personnel around the country, he held a dozen of training classes to promote the patent technology to the country, and further transform scientific research achievements into strong productivity. At the same time, it solved the problem that China had depended on import for a long time. Trainees were high-end talents of large enterprises.

In the great tides of reform and opening-up, Yingge had exerted his uttermost efforts to fight in the township enterprises, provided them with technologies and raw materials and enabled them to get technical support and help. Yingge had done his share to the development of township enterprises and had left innovative "footprints" on the development road of township enterprises, small and medium-sized enterprises.

Look back upon his past, Yingge was glad of his choices. At the retirement turning of his life, he didn't wander and give up; instead he proceeded to explore and move forward.

On January 15, 2009, Professor Yingge won the award of "Excellent Character in China's Reform" in Great Hall of the People in Beijing, and was cordially received by the Party and national leaders.

2. Ten Thousand Versus Three Million

It's warm and sunny in spring as winter just passed. Different concrete factories in Liaoning province were hectic. Director Gao of Majiazi Concrete Factory and his secretary suddenly came to Yingge's special alloy research institute. They seemed anxious and wanted to pick Yingge up to their factory. The cement kiln shut-down accident might lead to risks of closure and bankruptcy of the factory and was related with the living of over 200 staff of the factory.

Yingge asked, "Such severe accident happened. Why don't you go to the concrete scientific research institution or the concrete science research institute for help? They have experts and professors. "

Director Gao answered, "Don't talk about it. We went there and they checked but it's too difficult for them. They don't have relevant experience. It takes a long time and they are not sure they can find out the reasons. If so, it's better to spend several millions to build a new kiln. We are too busy in building a large kiln worth of dozens of million so we left."

Director Gao continued, "Later Director Wang of Xishan Concrete Factor suggested that we should ask your help. They had the same problem before." He said, "At that time, they were restless and didn't know what to do but you only repaired that in five days. Now it's still operating well and the concrete quality is good. Besides, the output is greater than before."

Director Wang also mentioned, "Professor Yingge is ready to help and doesn't put on expert airs. It only costs us 10,000 yuan. It's not expensive."

Director Gao told Yingge, "We can't find a way so we resort to you. Professor Yingge, please help us no matter how much it costs. We have over 200 employees."

Yingge said, "We don't take advantage of others when they are down. Usually it's 10,000 yuan which will be enough for materials. We don't overcharge. Let's go to the site."

After arriving at the site, Yingge found that it's a large mechanical shaft kiln which produced concrete rapidly. It's over 20m deep from the ground to underground with a capacity of over 30 tons. It seemed hard to solve it on the outside. The problem could only be located when you probed into the bottom of the kiln, that was, the depth of over 20m. Yingge said, "Put out the fire in the kiln first. Move all the materials in the kiln onto the ground. Empty the bottom. Then we can go down to check and analyze why it stops rotating so that we can decide what alloy materials and technologies should be used for repair. It's a new technology in metal surface engineering."

Director Gao and his secretary said, "Professor, you can't go down. It's over 20m deep. You are getting old and it's too dangerous for you to go down there by the rope ladder which will swing hard in the air. You might fall down and lose your life once you step empty. It's not cooled down yet inside the kiln. It's over 40℃. It's too hot. You can't stand it! So you can't go!"

Yingge said, "There's difficulty no matter what you do. It takes several days for the kiln to cool down completely. Won't it influence your production? I can't treat it casually since you are like ants on a hot pan."

Director Gao was so touched, "Professor Yingge, you are really our savior! Our factory has signed a contract with the construction company. We received their advance payment. If we don't deliver the goods on time and the quality is not as expected, we will be legally held accountable and compensate 3 million yuan for their losses."

Yingge was vexed, "Stop the fire right now and empty the kiln. I will go down to find out the reason."

Yingge did some preparation. He put on the outfit and went down along the rope ladder. It didn't cool off yet in the kiln so Yingge sweat a lot. The director used the fan to help him feel better. Yingge found out the reason for breakdown in a short time. Several teeth weren't well welded so they fell off and were stuck in the opening of feeding and blanking trays. Therefore, the unloading tray stopped working. Workers took out the teeth soon and repaired with the new alloy materials based on the new technology and process of Yingge. They wouldn't fall off again now.

Yingge proposed three new technologies: the teeth and the surface were fixed by high-strength metal materials; the area around was enveloped by materials with hot spray welding technology so as to achieve the effects of impact, wear-resisting and great hardness. Other teeth were sprayed with alloy as well to strengthen their solidness. Then a destructive test was conducted. They used a big hammer of 10 pounds to hit them to see whether they fell off or not. Only when there's no problem in this way could normal production be implemented.

Yingge said, "Now I am going to call our research institute to send relevant equipment and materials so that you can go down the kiln to repair it with my alloy materials according to my technology as soon as possible."

With the personal instruction of Yingge in the kiln within five days, the unloading trays metal surfaces were all repaired with wear-resisting technology. In the destructive test, tray teeth were fixed with alloy and they could stand impact and wear. Through half a year's operation, all of them met the requirements and the breakdown problem was solved. A new way was innovated and rich experience was obtained. Later, an invention patent was applied for. Since then, Yingge had left an arduous "footprint" of solving the problem of the shaft kiln and great productivity development of the building industry.

3. Brave Danger to Make New Breakthroughs

The application of large-area metal surface spray under constant temperature in large high temperature and wear-resisting power generation projects was the latest scientific research achievement made by Professor Yingge and his team in recent years. The invention patent was ZL01102869.6. It solved the international problem of constant temperature treatment of metal surface engineering and high temperature and wear-resisting production, thus making the application of fluidized bed boiler with high temperature and severe wear embrace a brand new opportunity after the down period.

Fluidized bed boiler was a kind of efficient and energy-saving high temperature boiler imported from abroad. The advantage was high thermal efficiency. The coal seam in the boiler was influenced by primary air and secondary air. The coal particles jump up and down in a high speed so they could be fully combusted. Its disadvantage was that due to the high speed circulation of the coal seam, the coal blocks and particles caused extremely severe frictions to the water pipes of the boiler. It would make the pipes leak and even explode in several months or half a year, thus leading to production suspension, gas suspension and power failure as well as severe losses and consequences to the production. Especially in winter, it would directly affect the heating and power supply of thousands of households.

Leaders, employees and technical personnel of many power generation factories and thermal power plants requested academician Yingge to solve the problems of quick wear of fluidized bed, severe heat corrosion and leakage & explosion of water pipes as soon as possible. The problem that the advanced boilers could be used but expensive to repair was an key internatinal technological one.

Yingge thought that since the factories proposed the request, it meant they trusted and entertained great expectation of him. As a scientific researcher of metal surface engineering, he should take it incumbent upon him to solve difficulties for them. Scientific researches served productivity.

He acted without delay. No matter how difficult it was, he would do it with his tough and persistent spirit. First, he did metal high temperature and wear-resisting experiments in the laboratory. The feature of metal materials was that they would become soft as long as they were heated. They would lose their hardness so it's likely to be worn out and oxidated under high temperature. The experiment temperature of Yingge varied from 1000°C to 2500°C. Different techniques were adopted such as surfacing, spray welding, flame spray, explosive spray, plasma spray, electric arc spray and large-area supersonic electric arc spray. Materials included powder, wire, nanometer, and multiple high-strength, corrosion and wear-resisting and high-temperature-proof alloy materials were developed. Different quality alloy materials were sprayed onto the 20# steel board for comparison and analysis. The hardness, stretching, strength and spray thickness were measured. In the end, a destructive test was conducted, that was, use a big hammer of twenty pounds to hit and test whether they would fall off or not. After plenty of practices and experiments, Yingge felt he's well prepared. He never fought a battle unprepared. When everything was ready, he and his students brought their experiment samples to Director Liu of a thermal power plant, and proposed to conduct wear-resisting and high temperature tests in the 3# boiler of the factory which was going to be repaired. He guaranteed that if wear-resisting treatment was conducted according to his plan, the problem of leakage and wear of the pipes wouldn't happen within two years. The director was so happy to hear that and said, "If what you said is true, you are making another great contribution to our country, Professor Yingge. There are over 3,000 boilers like this around the country. It costs over 20,000 yuan for starting the boiler once. The losses would be greater once it's stopped and the power and industrial gas were less produced. Hundreds of thousands of yuan would be lost in the least and millions of yuan would be lost to the uttermost. It's serious! Professor, your innovative technology saves us millions to dozens of millions yuan for us a year! Scientific researchers like you are the living wealth gods of factories." Yingge answered modestly, "It's obligatory to help you tide out difficulties."

Director Liu said solemnly, "Although your solution is good, I am not the one to make the decision. Tomorrow I will hold a leaders' meeting and invite Professor Yingge to take part in as an exception. You will explain your solution to them. If most of the leaders agree, we will start implementing it. It takes dozens of millions yuan and even hundreds of millions yuan to set up a boiler. We trust you, Professor Yingge. If it's somebody else, we won't let them test in the boiler at all and maybe we don't let them enter our factory. It's a foreign high technology which can't be randomly experimented. We don't trust other. Please understand us, Professor Yingge."

"I understand you, director." answered Yingge.

Professor Yingge lived in the VIP guesthouse of the factory. He didn't have time to watch TV at night. He started preparing for the meeting next day without having dinner and thought how to convince others. He re-integrated the data in the experiment, thought about questions that might be asked and was fully prepared for different opinions of others.

At the factory's leaders' meeting, Professor Yingge answered people's questions fluently with his unique personality charisma and the temperament of a performer. He convinced people with his scientific test data who unanimously agreed that wear-resisting tests were conducted in the 3# boiler. Some people said only extensive knowledge and talents led to genuine knowledge while brave acts and behaviors produced achievements. Yingge was a senior intellect who had extensive interests and was enterprising and well-informed. With the blood and nature of Shandong people, hesitation was not in his dictionary. He signed the success and failure contract on site. How much boldness of vision it took! Once he failed, he would shoulder economic responsibilities! He would go bankrupt if it's not that severe and be put into prison if it's bad. Yingge's hand was shaking while signing the contract. The signing of the contract indicated legal responsibilities! However..... He really feared after the event.

In the end, director Liu announced solemnly, "Since you agreed with the test solution of Professor Yingge, we would have the tests in the 3# boiler." Director Liu asked, "How many days does it take to prepare?" Yingge said, "Three days will do."

Director Liu patted Yingge, "You are really looking forward to it! Well! You won't take the job if you don't have an ace up your sleeve! You will be responsible for any accident and we will act according to the contract. Keep your word! Wish you a success!"

Yingge said, "Okay! Meet you at the 3# boiler at 9:00am, Thursday."

After coming back, Yingge thought it's a rare opportunity because he had contacted several thermal power plants before but failed to reach an agreement. Those power factories valued economic benefits and were reluctant to be the first one to try tomatoes. They demandingly requested success only.

Before the experiment, Yingge prepared actively in material, spiritual and technological aspects. In the past few days, he had been busy like a bee.

Even if Yingge had been fully prepared in spiritual aspect, he was still restless in the past few days and he was thinner...... He realized rationally that it's not like the laboratory for which success or failure didn't matter. It's for real this time. If he screwed up this time, he would compensate economically for losses as agreed in the contract.

Yingge came to the site on time on Thursday. Director Liu, General Manager Wu, Mr. Zhou, head of boiler production department and director Zhuang of the power plant arrived at the site. Yingge was studying the construction plan with his students and workers. The power generation boiler was huge. The inside was 15 square meters and it's over 40m from the bottom to the chimney, which was equivalent to a ten-storied building. When you looked down from the top, you would feel fainted. Researchers must enter inside the boiler from the top and they had to climb a rope ladder of 37m to get to the top. It's a severe challenge for academician Yingge who was over 70 years old to climb the ladder. Director Liu, deputy director Sun, General Manager Wu and students didn't want Professor Yingge to take the great risk. After all, he's old and a bit physically disabled. Once the accident happened, the consequences would be inconceivable.

Yingge convinced them with his sincerity and determination.

Yingge said seriously, "I made the test solution and studied the wear-resisting alloy and construction processes. It's a hard-won test opportunity and we have signed the contract. There's risk and difficulties for all jobs. I can't flinch at crucial junctures. I have to act! It's inappropriate to let my students to bear the risk for me. There's danger and failure if you are engaged in key scientific research projects. Good technology and good ideologies are not enough for scientific researches with risks. At crucial moments, you need to have the sacrifice spirit and be brave to do something that hasn't been done before just like Nobel who risked his life to test the explosives and Franklin who risked his life to test the thundering and explore scientific data in the rains. Although they sacrificed their lives to the science cause, they would forever live in the minds of people in the world."

Yingge continued, "Yang Liwei, the first aerospace man of China, performed his task without being worried about his life. At that time, he didn't think he would come back to earth alive. Their performance would be recorded in the history forever. The following scientists won't go to the moon to reveal the mystery of the universe but for his pioneering example."

Academician Yingge finally convinced them. Watched by them, Yingge climbed it in a brave and arduous way. When he completed over 20m of it, most of his stamina had been consumed

and his legs got numb and waist twisted. It's getting harder and harder and his breath was shorter and shorter. The swing degree of the ladder was greater in the air. Suddenly one of his feet trembled and left the ladder. How dangerous it was! He rapidly grasped the rope with his hands and didn't fall off. People watching him under the boiler were in cold sweats.

Yingge thought to himself: Hang in there! Don't be afraid. Don't fall off. He ground his teeth and looked upwards instead of downwards. Yingge felt dizzy due to his high blood pressure but he insisted! Finally, 10m, 8m, 5m and 3m. He saw a glimpse of hope. 2m, 1m...... He finally overcame himself and reached the top. A man of over 70 years old conquered the height of 37m. People underneath exhaled and were relieved, and then warmly applauded the successful old man.

He now experienced the taste of climbing the top with bitterness, danger and happiness. He had left a strip of shining "footprints" in the processing of climbing the top.

Later on, Zhao Liang, one of his students, entered the boiler as well for detailed operation. Three students had successively climbed onto the 37m rope ladder under the encouragement of their teacher, and successfully entered the boiler from the top. Then Mr. Zhou, a young man, climbed the ladder and supervised from the top.

With the command of Yingge, they observed the spray temperature while recording all outcome and data from 1,200°C, 1,800°C, 2,000°C and 2,200°C to 2,500°C and 3,000°C. Students shouted "stop"; otherwise it would explode. Yingge actually applied the optimum seeking method of the great mathematician Loo-Keng Hua and found the best spray temperature and high-temperature alloy. In order to let followers obtain safe scientific data, Yingge provided key data. His arduous climbing finally paid off and key scientific research achievements had been obtained. It laid theoretical and practical foundations for high temperature and wear-resisting and corrosion-resisting of heat spray boiler pipes. With his rigorous scientific attitude, Yingge ignored the risks of explosion and eventually acquired reliable parameters so that followers would be safe. He had successfully completed the spray processes with high temperature and wear-resisting tests. Yingge set a pioneering example in high temperature and wear-resisting field and solved the bottleneck problem of being easy to be worn and hard to repair in the middle and top parts of the foreign and domestic high temperature power generation boilers during the production. He secured important safety data for future high altitude, high pressure and high temperature spray as well as wear and corrosion-resisting, and found out the technical data for prolonging the service life of boilers.

Through a year and a half's continuous high temperature and heavy load production operation in the power plant, they powerfully proved that Yingge's innovative high temperature and wear-resisting technology in the operation was reliable and the service life of the boiler was prolonged with good heat-conducting property and strong alloy surface combination. It's also characterized by non-peeling, non-falling, smooth surfaces, no current wear and high heat efficiency. It's helpful to energy-saving and emission reduction. The selected alloy could resist high temperature, corrosion and wear. The scientific test met with advanced international standards.

In the past, it needed to be stopped and overhauled once every few months or once very few weeks. Power and gas failure brought huge losses and inconvenience to thermal power production and people's life. Especially in winter, people would suffer a lot due to boiler overhaul, power and gas failure.

Now the boiler was still safe and reliable after three years' operation, which brought about benefits of several times greater to the thermal power production. It's a miracle created by academician Yingge by risking his life. It's approved as an invention patent by the national government. The patent technology was soon promoted and applied in Shandong, Hebei, Henan, Inner Mongolia, three provinces in Northeast China and other places around the country. Scientific research achievements were transformed into strong productivity. It's regarded by thermal power plants as "a green and environmental friendly technology". So far, it had been promoted around the country without declining over the years. Therefore, at the 16th International Metal Surface

Spray Exchange Meeting, Yingge's academic report was well reviewed by foreign experts of the same profession.

Allen Read, academician of Canadian Academy of Sciences and chairman of the meeting, and Professor Beer, academician of British Royal Academy of Sciences, commented, "Your scientific research achievements opened up a new field for metal high temperature and wear-resisting and the application of constant temperature spray under high temperature in the world. Besides, new enlightenment was provided. It's quite valuable......"

It's not only a great evaluation of Yingge's "enthusiastic life" and his "ambition" of transcending himself but also an appreciation of Chinese scientists' unremitting efforts in the field.

Just like all other scientists, Yingge was patriotic but he had unique "persistence" under the support of which he could put aside his life to go beyond limits and realize his dream with a sacrifice spirit. It's the source of his successive successes.

The sacrifice spirit of Yingge was not possessed by every scholar. It's hard to reach such a realm but for endless loyalty to the scientific research cause of the motherland and the Party, consistent strict requirements, self-attainment and forget-everything in scientific research practices. He's the model whom young scientists should learn from.

The year of 2009 was the 60th birthday of our motherland and a time when Yingge achieved great success in his career. On March 31, 2009, in the auditorium of Dalian Municipal Committee, Yingge won Science and Technology Invention Award of Dalian; in September, 2009, he won the honorable title of "Outstanding Inventor" and certificate of Dalian.

What's more respectable was that Yingge donated tens of thousands of scientific research bonus and academician funds of memorial significance to the university without reservation. With his kind move, he helped teachers, students and retired senior leaders who were in difficulty. It's because he was a person who knew how to repay others' favor. He had repaid Jiaotong University where he worked and grew with his performances.

In 2008 when the earthquake attacked Wenchuan, although Yingge was seriously ill in bed, he asked his wife to donate 5,000 yuan to the disaster relief office first time. Among all people in the retirement office, Yingge donated most and most timely because he would never forget those who once helped him and those who needed his help as well. It's an expert's due quality to do something for suffering fellows. Yingge's good deed was published in the journal of Jiaotong University.

As Mr. Yingge was getting better, he started developing different types of wear and corrosion-resisting alloy materials as demanded by the production of power plants. Those materials could be applied on different occasions such as mechanics, chemistry industry, metallurgy, mining, surface ship, freight vessels, airplanes, military vehicles, tanks, nuclear submarines, propellers and other spare parts. Different alloys which he studied could be used to repair wasted equipments. It's attractive in both quality and price. Its repair cost was only 1/10 to 1/20 of the original price but it's better in strength and endurance. Plenty of steel, bronze and non-ferrous metals were saved for the country. His wear-resisting technology, be it high temperature wear-resisting or low temperature wear-resisting, was approved by domestic and foreign experts.

In June, 2010, Yingge was invited to attend the academic seminar for military equipment emergency repair held by Office of the National Defense Industry in Dalian. His paper was included in the collection of army emergency repair essays. Besides, he made an academic report which was appreciated by experts inside and outside the army circle.

4. He's at the Far End of the Street Where the Candlelight Was the Dimmest

Wang Guowei, a modern scholar of China, was a well-known former professor of Chinese ancient civilization of Huaqing University, concluded three realms of successful people in a very vivid way. It's quite suitable for the fighting experience of academician Yingge:

"Westerly winds withered trees up last night. Climbing up the stairs and being lonely on the loft, I overlooked the endless distance." It's the first realm.

"For you I am pining myself away without regret." It's the second realm.

"Having almost exhausted my energy searching for that person (vague), I suddenly turned my head, and there they were, standing at the far end of the street where the candlelight is the dimmest." This was the third realm.

It's because he had a grand ideal that he could climb the towering building which was seldom visited alone when "westerly winds withered trees up", have a right insight into the road ahead, looked far ahead and aimed high.

The indulging and forget-everything spiritual realm of "For you I am pining myself away without regret." made it definite to achieve success and reach his goals in his lifetime.

He finally had his dream of life come true and climbed onto the peak of the science field-- the title of academician. He couldn't be found in the crown but the far end of the street where the candlelight was the dimmest. Even if he reached the peak in both his career and his life, he never showed it off; instead, he was silently contributing. Some old comrades asked when they met each other, "Haven't seen you for years. Why do you make yourself so busy? You already have too many scientific research achievements."

Although Yingge was not as great as Nobel, Franklin and Yang Liwei and couldn't be compared with them, his braveness and persistence in his cause made people admirable in awe.

Yingge always followed three principles in conducting himself and dealing with matters: first, make a living on technological innovation; second, make a living on being realistic and practical; third, make a living on following tightly the Party. As long as the flag of scientific outlook on development was held high, the "footprints" of his would be definitely on the shining road to success.

As an academician, Yingge had realized his perfect life, made contributions to the country with his unremitting efforts, and always kept the principle of being modest and prudent, and guarding against arrogance and impatience. He possessed three national invention patents and four high-tech achievements which had been transformed to strong productivity. He had made four technological innovations with four corporate management strategies. The special alloy research team which he set up won Best Management Achievement Award at the 10th World Conference on Management Science. He was elected as the vice president of Chinese nationality at the World Conference on Management Science held in Paris, France, which was the first time a Chinese won the honorable title. His invention patents had solved difficulties in power generation. In the 6th Assessment of Theory and Practice Achievements in Developing Advanced Productivity around the Country, he won Special Prize in Outstanding Contribution in developing advanced productivity around the country. He won "Excellent Character in China's Reforms" in Great Hall of the People in Beijing, and a "'Five-star' Quality Medal for Outstanding Achievements in the Construction of the People's Republic of China" awarded by Chinese Academy of Management Science. Besides, he was hired as the honorable president and lifetime professor by International Academy of Sciences. He also served as the editorial board member of China's metal hard surface technology journal and the honorable editorial board member of Commercial Press in North America. These shining honors demonstrated that Yingge was a versatile and talented outstanding expert and master who never showed off his reputation and successes around.

Yingge said, "He will feel no compunction only when he's indifferent to fame and wealth, maintain a peaceful mind, care about others and show respect for others, would rather let other benefits than benefiting himself. Among all kinds of recipes, only a peaceful mind is a healthy one. Only when you bear a peaceful mind can you enjoy your meals, have good sleeps, laugh safe laughters, live a comfortable and long life."

Yingge often remarked, "Marx is so great but he only has one best friend in his life who is Engels. The friendship between them is the model for human beings. It demonstrates that it's easy to earn gold and silver but hard to make a bosom friend. When you water flowers, you water their roots. When you make friends, you must be honest. He always treats his friends with sincerity and cordiality."

Yingge always bore in mind that the management of his alloy research institute and the enterprise all came down to the management of people. He always stuck to the people-oriented management philosophy. Hence, he always took the lead in corporate management. From the inception of the establishment of his research institute to present, its value had been increased all the way to millions and even hundreds of millions yuan from ten thousand yuan.

5. Strategy-- the Treasure of Success in Corporate Management

Strategy was the treasure of success in corporate management. Yingge maintained that the development of advanced productivity was inseparable from scientific corporate management. Benefits should be emphasized and the source of benefits was management of people in the final analysis. High quality people brought about high quality enterprises and high economic benefits. Therefore, they should spare no effort to train employees about their qualities so that each of them could become an elite of the research institute. The success of an enterprise mainly relied on the right "people-oriented" strategy formulated by leaders. Yingge also read Master Sun's Art of War carefully and applied ancient military strategies to modern corporate management. Some people said it's an innovative move in modern corporate management.

Yingge had always combined corporate management and ideologies of conducting oneself with employees' immediate interests.

The philosophical opinion of Marxism held that material was the primary and spirit was secondary. He let employees understand that the management means and systems of an enterprise were formulated to develop the enterprise, improve benefits and earn the greatest benefits for employees. As corporate benefits increased, so it's with the income of employees. Just as the ancient saying went, "when large rivers are full, branches are full as well and when the water rises, the boat floats."

When employees understood it, they would regard corporate interest as their code of conduct, transform enterprises' "system management" to "self-management" of employees, and transcend "themselves". By management, it didn't mean to let them "follow orders" and "be obedient"; instead their conscious actions and results during the production should be examined. Both the "root" and the "surface" should be emphasized. As long as one thing was favorable to an enterprise, it's beneficial to its employees and employees would compete to deal with the thing. Rescuing the enterprise at a snow night was a case in point.

One sunny winter day in 2008, dozens of boxes of valuable imported metal powder and dozens of boxes of special welded alloy bars were placed in the courtyard of the research institute for drying. It's good weather so they weren't collected in the evening.

However, something was unpredictable. It suddenly snowed at night. The wind, snow and rain were the order and the emergency was the call. Employees happened to rush towards the factory together at the snowy, windy and rainy night. Some of them even brought their families for the rescue. Some of their used their own shoulders and some used the vehicles. Soon the boxes were collected and over a million of economic losses was avoided for the enterprise.

Yingge exclaimed, "What kind of spirit is it? They regard the research institute as their home, which is the spirit. What kind of strength is it? It's the strength of self management. It's a success in the people-oriented management strategy and transformation of spirit to material. What respectable employees! How lofty their spirit of ownership! How admirable and moving it is!" Next day, Yingge gave each of them 500 yuan to reward their lofty spirit of ownership and motivated their greater potential.

Strategic management of an enterprise was to let employees and the enterprise to breathe the same air, share the same fate and in perfect sympathy with each other. It's meant to let them put their heads together for the same goal and reach the realm of being proud for the prosperity of the institute and managing themselves.

"Don't mention difficulties. It's because there's difficulty that you are asked to solve it. Difficulties have to be confronted whether there are favorable conditions or not." It's the code of conduct for employees and also the new realm for self management conducted by the institute. First, it's the due personality charisma of entrepreneurs who should set an example for employees instead of talking only, and work out new management strategies and measures. Different strategies should be implemented at different periods:

Just as Suvorov, great Russian Marshal said, "Discipline is the mother of victory and the most important thing in the world. There's no progress without discipline and there's no quality without discipline..."

The great Indian writer Tagore remarked, "God's right hand is gentle while his left hand goes hard."

Great French General Napoleon said, "We use our left brain to obey while using right brain to create."

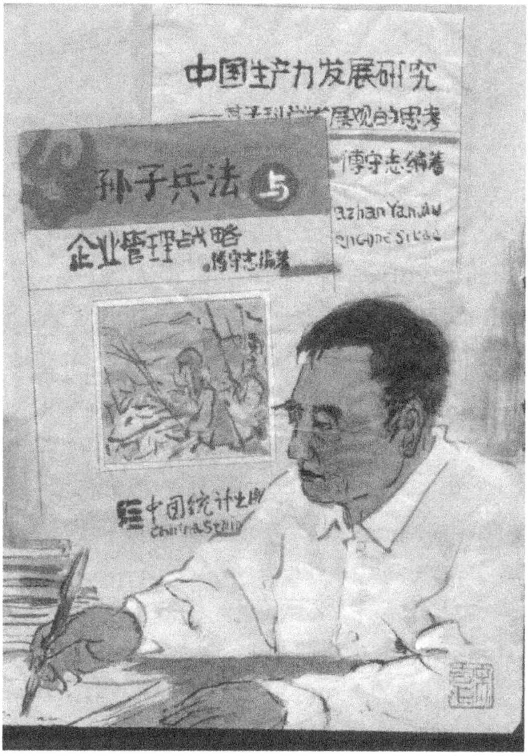

The strategy developed by the institute requested employees to follow sheer disciplines, labor innovatively, act consciously, manage themselves and turn passiveness into activeness.

Yingge was good at transpositional consideration and reverse thinking. China had a splendid civilization of thousands of years. 2,500 years ago, many saints such as Sun Zi, Confucius, Lao-tse and Mo-tse had proved themselves to be outstanding militarists, educators, philosophers and scientists at that time. What if Sun Zi studied enterprises instead of military strategies? What if Zhuge Liang didn't command battles but served as General Manager of an enterprise? According to such hypotheses, Yingge concluded that great minds thought alike. Hence, he completed his book of *Master Sun's Arts of War and Corporate Management Strategies* based on his successful experience in corporate management over the past 20-odd years which was spoken highly of by international friends at the World Conference on Management Science held in France and enabled foreigners to realize the fact that China already developed modern military management science earlier 2,500 years ago. American entrepreneurs showed great interest in this book at the conference and suggested it should be published by the well-known Commercial Press of America in English and further released around the world.

6. Elected as Vice President of WAPS

In July, 2010, Mr. Yingge was invited to attend the 10th World Conference on Management Science held in Paris, France, as a member of Chinese delegate, and made an important speech at the conference. With his sonorous voice, clear articulation of words and citation of various authorities, he talked about excitedly about splendid ancient Chinese culture and applied the military strategies in *Master Sun's Arts of War* 2,500 years ago to modern scientific corporate management. He took his own research institute as an example, and introduced to the world the military strategies of "winning the strong with the weak", "winning the majority with the minority", "attacking the weak with the strong", "avoiding the strong and attacking the weak" and "Knowing the enemy and yourself, you can fight a hundred battles and win them all", etc. which were used in modern corporate management. His excellent speech was a revelation to foreign and domestic experts present and shocked the entire audience. He won a long standing ovation and won glories for Chinese people on the international arena.

In the past, it's believed in the west that China needed to learn from foreign countries in terms of corporate management such as Japan, America, Germany and France, and Chinese people didn't have their own management science and theories. At the conference, he showed foreign and domestic experts China's splendid military management science 2,500 years ago, and China was the birthplace of the world's civilization. His speech was praised by the world's experts. Hence, at the conference, he was honorably elected as the vice president of Chinese nationality. It's unprecedented. Yingge was the first vice president of Chinese nationality at the conference who had the right to make the speech in leading the world and was the "first person" winning glories for Chinese people!

What's worth mentioning was that his paper which combined scientific management and productivity was assessed as "Best Contribution Award of China's Corporate Management in the World's Management Science" at the conference!

Since then, he had left the footprint of winning glories for the country at the international science arena.

Yingge wore deep blue suit, white shirt, red tie and nameplate with the sign of vice president on it, brown Italian leather shoes and light color glasses. Professor Braider, executive president of the conference, shouted, "Let's welcome vice president Yingge from China's Dalian Jiaotong University to make a report." He's so excited to hear the name of Jiaotong University on the world's science arena. He treated Jiaotong University as his mother and he's her loyal son. Stepping on the rostrum of the conference, he said with his unique personality charisma and temperament of an orator, "Ladies and gentlemen! Dear friends! Over 600 representatives coming from five continents of the world gathered in Paris, beautiful capital of France, to attend this conference. It will leave you and me an unforgettable and beautiful memory. First, as the vice president of the conference, I would like to wish you 'Good morning' and the conference a success!" As he was finished, a storm of applause was heard.

His topic was "Strategy Is the Treasure of Success in Corporate Management". His speech was constantly interrupted by bursts of applause. It's an unforgettable scene of Chinese people on the world's rostrum. He won glories and honors for Chinese people. He was equal to the title of vice president, which proved that he had the ability and talent of leading the world on the science arena. His report essay was assessed as Excellent Essay First Prize and won the certificate. His essay was translated into English to be handed to representatives of different countries and was unanimously praised by foreign scholars. He had left the “footprint” of winning glories for Chinese people on the rostrum of World Conference on Science Management.

Due to Yingge’s unremitting efforts, abundant achievements and phenomenal performance, his another book *Study on Development of China's Productivity-- Thought Based on Scientific Outlook on Development* was published by National Economic Science Press and released by Xinhua Bookstore. It’s the crystallization of his painstaking efforts. For years, he had made outstanding contribution to the development of China’s advanced productivity. Through the assessment and declaration of Academician Committee of China’s Productivity Society of WAPS, the 16th WAPS Conference held in Antalya, Turkey, on November 2, 2010, was held and at the conference, foreign academicians voted and agreed unanimously to award Yingge the title of academician of WAPS. The certificate and medal was jointly awarded by President Thomas Tuttle and academician John Heap, president of United Nation’s WAPS League. It’s another outcome brought about by Yingge’s braveness in taking the lead and living an enthusiastic life as well as climbing the peaks of the world’s science. He won glories again for Chinese people at the conference. Yingge said, “As an ordinary teacher, the acquirement of these performances and achievements were finally attributed to the instructions of the Party, the training of university leaders, teachers’ help, support of comrades and profound love of students in the past years. I would like to mention my favorite words, ‘Glories belong to Jiaotong University. No matter how tall the tree grows, it won’t forget its root.’”

In December, 2011, the leader of Dalian CPPCC announced at the Party’s representatives conference: Comrade Yingge from Jiaotong University, an excellent Party member, was invited to attend the World Conference on Science Management held in Paris,

France, as a member of Chinese delegate, and he was elected as the vice president of Chinese nationality. It's the glory of Dalian. He made academic exchanges in foreign countries such as Turkey, Paris of France, Austria, Switzerland, Sweden, Italy and Germany, and had left the 'footprint' of academician Yingge.

After being promoted to an academician, he felt his burden was greater. He had survived several narrow escapes for the sake of the scientific research cause. In an auspicious era, he's contented to have the opportunity to fight and make new contributions to the country and people. He was happy. People were contented when the matters were satisfying while people's quality was naturally great if they were selfless. He was a warrior who kept fighting and whose mood wouldn't be affected by the good or bad status of external things. He's a wise man and brave man whose fate was closely connected with the era. Although he's old, he still aimed the scientific research goal at the difficulties in the world's scientific researches such as development of low-carbon economy and circular economy, promotion of energy-saving and emission reduction, building of a harmonious ecological environment. It's the solemn pledge of Premier Wen at the Copenhagen Conference. Hence, China should make greater contributions to the world......

As an academician, it's Mr. Yingge's greatest wish to remove anxiety of the country and do his share to the country. Although he's almost 80, the title of academician was not his finishing line but a new starting point for him, and the second golden age for him to repay the Party and university. He's completely devoted to a pioneering scientific research project: he designed a Taichi combustion reactor based on the symmetry and balance principle in the Taichi diagram of Yin and Yang in ancient China. With the principle of catalyst, CO_2 in high temperature smoke was disassembled into CO for combustion, and then sprayed into the boiler under high temperature. It's turned into treasure from waste and benefits from harm, thus saving 30% of the energy. After dynamic balance, the discharged CO2 was greatly reduced. The new technology of energy-saving and emission reduction with Chinese characteristics was bound to make greater contributions to human beings. SO2 was an important chemical substance which accounted for acid rain and damaged crops. Besides, it's extremely harmful to people's health.

According to the chemical principle of catalytic deoxidizing reaction, Yingge restored the sulfur element in SO2 to elemental sulfur. The noxious substance discharged from the boiler: SO2+2MS=3S+2MO. The recycled elemental sulfur was calculated based on one yuan/kg, a wealth of 200 billion yuan could be recovered every year. It's the development of circular economy to conduct energy-saving and emission reduction with re-use. In March, 2012, it's approved as a national innovation project to apply for invention patent at the China's High-tech Industrialization Seminar in Beijing. Yingge's "footprints" of exploration in his enthusiastic life were worth our further expectation!

The introduction of high technologies had built Yingge's career glories. Much as he's reached his career peak and overlooked all top scenery, he still had a more perfect life to materialize.

It could be concluded as follows:

Although he's old, he's ambitious,
He acted out the scientific outlook on development,
His footprints had been shining all the way,
He encouraged the later generation to climb new heights!

7. Ardent Wish of the Old Secretary

In July, 2011, Sun Yongchun, the former Party Secretary of Jiaotong University, came to Dalian to visit his former subordinates and old professors of the university, and received academician Yingge separately in Yingge's office. Mr. Sun who bore the Party's instructions on mind had never separated from the public, often cared about comrades and the development of scientific research achievements. Yingge was happy to see his amiable, respectable, prestigious old leader who looked far and aimed high and had been frank and forthright in his life was healthy and enthusiastic. After hugging each other cordially, the old secretary asked about details and cared about him. Seeing the myriads of certificates and scrolls, especially Yingge's certificate and medal of WAPS academician, he kept saying, "Awesome! Great! You have won so many national and global awards. It means you are qualified for the academician title. Our university finally had an academician, which demonstrates that Jiaotong University is developing and growing stronger. Her reputation will be expanded. You won glories for our university."

"Jiaotong University is like a crown and the academician honor is like the bright pearl on the crown. You must cherish the lofty honor of academician title. In future, our university will have the second, third....even more academicians. Only in this way can our university get better."

"It's worth celebrating and publicizing! Wish you achieve greater success with your academician functions!"

Upon close contact with Yingge, we couldn't help admiring him. His unknown efforts and uplifting progress, responsibilities for his career, his esteem, his braveness, his selflessness, his uttermost efforts, his sacrifice spirit and his numerous scientific research achievements constitute the most beautiful symphony of his life. His footprints would be valuable spiritual wealth both at present and in future, and were unforgettable to people.

Made in the USA
Monee, IL
05 November 2026

67808609R00118